Arizona Diamondbacks 2019

A Baseball Companion

Edited by Patrick Dubuque, Aaron Gleeman and Bret Sayre

Baseball Prospectus

Craig Brown and Dave Pease, Consultant Editors
Rob McQuown and Harry Pavlidis, Statistics Editors

Copyright © 2019 by DIY Baseball, LLC.
All rights reserved

This book or any part thereof may not be reproduced or transmitted in any form or by any means, electronic or mechanical, including photocopying, recording, or by any information storage and retrieval system, without permission in writing from the publisher.

Limit of Liability/Disclaimer of Warranty: While the publisher and the author have used their best efforts in preparing this book, they make no representations or warranties with respect to the accuracy or completeness of the contents of this book and specifically disclaim any implied warranties of merchantability or fitness for a particular purpose. No warranty may be created or extended by sales representatives or written sales materials. The advice and strategies contained herein may not be suitable for your situation. You should consult with a professional where appropriate. Neither the publisher nor the author shall be liable for any loss of profit or any other commercial damages, including but not limited to special, incidental, consequential, or other damages.

Library of Congress Cataloging-in-Publication Data:
paperback
ISBN-13: 978-1-949332-30-8

Project Credits
Cover Design: Kathleen Dyson
Interior Design and Production: Jeff Pease, Dave Pease
Layout: Jeff Pease, Dave Pease

Baseball icon courtesy of Uberux, from https://www.shareicon.net/author/uberux

Ballpark diagram courtesy of Lou Spirito/THIRTY81 Project, https://thirty81project.com/

Manufactured in the United States of America
10 9 8 7 6 5 4 3 2 1

Table of Contents

Foreword v
    Rob Mains

Statistical Introduction vii

Part 1: Team Analysis

Table for Two: Previewing the 2019 Arizona Diamondbacks 3
    Randy Holt and Jeff Wiser

Performance Graphs 7

2018 Team Performance 8

2019 Team Projections 9

Team Personnel 10

Chase Field Stats 11

Diamondbacks Team Analysis 13

Part 2: Player Analysis

Diamondbacks Player Analysis 20

Diamondbacks Prospects 89

Part 3: Featured Articles

The Hole in The Shift is Fixing Itself 101
    Russell Carleton

The State of the Quality Start 105
    Rob Mains

Heads-Up Hacking—The First Pitch 111
    Matthew Trueblood

A Hymn for the Index Stat 117
    Patrick Dubuque

Index of Names 121

Foreword

Rob Mains

Welcome to this companion of the 2019 Arizona Diamondbacks. We at Baseball Prospectus are excited to provide this analysis of the Diamondbacks.

Our website, Baseball Prospectus, is a leader in delivering high-quality commentary and data to baseball fans everywhere. To some, those words—commentary and data—appear mutually exclusive. There are people out there who believe that traditional analysis and advanced analytics must run on different paths. But the simplistic narrative of stats vs. traditionalists just isn't true. Every team's analytics department interacts with scouting, development, and major league operations with a common goal: Delivering a championship. New technologies, like radar tracking of pitch speeds and movement, enable talent evaluators to focus on qualitative aspects of pitching like mechanics and pitch sequencing. In-game strategies like infield shifts, based on batters' hit tendencies, help turn balls in play into outs. Hitters use information to adjust their swings to maximize run production.

All these numbers can seem, at best, intimidating, and at worst, counterproductive to the casual fan. Even as technology and analysis have embedded themselves deeply into the way teams run, it can often feel like statistics create a displacement between the viewer and the sport, breaking them out of the action. And yet every fan incorporates the numbers to some degree; stats like batting average and earned run average, so fundamental to how we talk about performance, are actually complicated formulas. They don't bother people because those formulas have become second nature, as easy to translate as the action on the field.

Along the way, new statistics have entered baseball's lexicon. You'll see some of them, like on-base percentage (which measures a batter's ability to get on base via walk, hit batter, or hit), OPS (on-base plus slugging), and average exit velocity (the speed of balls off a hitter's bat) on broadcasts. Others, like DRC+, might well be new to you. Some of them have been well-defined to the public, others haven't. That lack of context has created ambiguity. Fans know that a ball hit 100 mph is scorched, but does that mean extra bases? (Not if it's hit on the ground or high in the air it doesn't.)

For those who are amenable to them, the new statistics can increase the enjoyment and understanding of the game. They can help fans identify when a pitcher is tiring, when a stolen base or a bunt attempt makes sense (and, more often, when it doesn't), or how a team's lineup might be constructed. Websites like Baseball Prospectus add to that understanding by weaving metrics into the narrative of the game. That's the goal of this publication: to take some of the newer, more complicated statistics and make them as intuitive as the ones on the back of old baseball cards.

But you don't need to love analytics to love baseball. The fans at BP who worked together to write this guide are captivated first and foremost by the game itself. We're drawn to Aaron Judge's power, Francisco Lindor's glove, Billy Hamilton's speed and Patrick Corbin's slider and don't need numbers to tell us why they're so mesmerizing. The underlying statistics provide depth to the game that we all love.

We hope you'll find that this guide helps you better understand the Diamondbacks. Our analysts have studied the team's major league personnel and its minor league affiliates to identify their strengths and weaknesses, both the obvious ones and those that only a careful dissection of players' performances—yes, including the data—can reveal. You don't need us to tell you who was good and who wasn't in 2018, but our models and writers can help you project how each player is going to perform this year and beyond, and appreciate the greatness of each new game as it unfolds. As in the sport itself, the human and analytic components combine to generate a deeper overall understanding.

Think back to the first time you saw a baseball game on a high-definition TV. You'd grown familiar with how the game looked and felt on a picture tube. But new TV allowed you to see details that you'd never seen before. That's how advanced statistics work. The game itself is why you're here and why you're buying this. (And, for that matter, why we wrote it.) The statistical measures provide the sharper focus, the detail, the depth of knowledge that you didn't have before, generating an overall superior picture. Enjoy the view.

—Rob Mains is an author of Baseball Prospectus.

Statistical Introduction

Sports are, fundamentally, a blend of athletic endeavor and storytelling. Baseball, like any other sport, tells its stories in so many ways: in the arc of a game from the stands or a season from the box scores, in photos, or even in numbers. At Baseball Prospectus, we understand that statistics don't replace observation or any of baseball's stories, but complement everything else that makes the game so much fun.

What stats help us with is with patterns and precision, variance and value. This book can help you learn things you may not see from watching a game or hundred, whether it's the path of a career over time or the breadth of the entire MLB. We'd also never ask you to choose between our numbers and the experience of viewing a game from the cheap seats or the comfort of your home; our publication combines running the numbers with observations and wisdom from some of the brightest minds we can find. But if you *do* want to learn more about the numbers beyond what's on the backs of player jerseys, let us help explain.

Offense

At the end of this past year, we've revised our methodology for determining batting value. Long-time readers of Baseball Prospectus will notice that we've retired True Average in favor of a new metric: Deserved Runs Created Plus (DRC+). Developed by Jonathan Judge and our stats team, this statistic measures everything a player does at the plate–reaching base, hitting for power, making outs, and moving runners over–and puts it on a scale where 100 equals league-average performance. A DRC+ of 150 is terrific, a DRC+ of 100 is average, and a DRC+ of 75 means you better be an excellent defender.

DRC+ also does a better job than any of our previous metrics in taking contextual factors into account. The model adjusts for how the park affects performance, but also for things like the talent of the opposing pitcher, value of different types of batted-ball events, league, temperature, and other factors. It's able to describe a player's expected offensive contribution than any other statistic we've found over the years, and also does a better job of predicting future performance as well.

The other aspect of run-scoring is baserunning, which we quantify using Baserunning Runs. BRR not only records the value of stolen bases (or getting caught in the act), but also accounts for a runner's ability to go first to third on a single or advance on a fly ball.

Defense

Where offensive value is *relatively* easy to identify and understand, defensive value is … not. Over the past dozen years, the sabermetric community has focused mostly on stats based on zone data: a real-live human person records the type of batted ball and estimated landing location, and models are created that give expected outs. From there, you can compare fielders' actual outs to those expected ones. Simple, right?

Unfortunately, zone data has two major issues. First, zone data is recorded by commercial data providers who keep the raw data private unless you pay for it. (All the statistics we build in this book and on our website use public data as inputs.) That hurts our ability to test assumptions or duplicate results. Second, over the years it has become apparent that there's quite a bit of "noise" in zone-based fielding analysis. Sometimes the conclusions drawn from zone data don't hold up to scrutiny, and sometimes the different data provided by different providers don't look anything alike, giving wildly different results. Sometimes the hard-working professional stringers or scorers might unknowingly inflict unconscious bias into the mix: for example good fielders will often be credited with more expected outs despite the data, and ballparks with high press boxes tend to score more line drives than ones with a lower press box.

Enter our Fielding Runs Above Average (FRAA). For most positions, FRAA is built from play-by-play data, which allows us to avoid the subjectivity found in many other fielding metrics. The idea is this: count how many fielding plays are made by a given player and compare that to expected plays for an average fielder at their position (based on pitcher ground-ball tendencies and batter handedness). Then we adjust for park and base-out situations.

When it comes to catchers, our methodology is a little different thanks to the laundry list of responsibilities they're tasked with beyond just, well, catching and throwing the ball. By now you've probably heard about "framing" or the art of making umpires more likely to call balls outside the strike zone for strikes. To put this into one tidy number, we incorporate pitch tracking data (for the years it exists) and adjust for important factors like pitcher, umpire, batter, and home-field advantage using a mixed-model approach. This grants us a number for how many strikes the catcher is personally adding to (or subtracting from) his pitchers' performance … which we then convert to runs added or lost using linear weights.

Framing is one of the biggest parts of determining catcher value, but we also take into account blocking balls from going past, whether a scorer deems it a passed ball or a wild pitch. We use a similar approach–one that really benefits from the pitch tracking data that tells us what ends up in the dirt and what doesn't. We also include a catcher's ability to prevent stolen bases and how well they field balls in play, and *finally* we come up with our FRAA for catchers.

Pitching

Both pitching and fielding make up the half of baseball that isn't run scoring: run prevention. Separating pitching from fielding is a tough task, and most recent pitching analysis has branched off from Voros McCracken's famous (and controversial) statement, "There is little if any difference among major-league pitchers in their ability to prevent hits on balls hit in the field of play." The research of the analytic community has validated this to some extent, and there are a host of "defense-independent" pitching measures that have been developed to try and extricate the effect of the defense behind a hurler from the pitcher's work.

Our solution to this quandry is Deserved Run Average (DRA), our core pitching metric. DRA looks like earned run average (ERA), the tried-and-true pitching stat you've seen on every baseball broadcast or box score from the past century, but it's very different. To start, DRA takes an event-by-event look at what the pitchers does, and adjusts the value of that event based on different environmental factors like park, batter, catcher, umpire, base-out situation, run differential, inning, defense, home field advantage, pitcher role, and temperature. That mixed model gives us a pitcher's expected contribution, similar to what we do for our DRC+ model for hitters and FRAA model for catchers. (Oh, and we also consider the pitcher's effect on basestealing and on balls getting past the catcher.)

It's important to note that DRA is set to the scale of runs allowed per nine innings (RA9) instead of ERA, which makes DRA's scale slightly higher than ERA's. The reason for this is because ERA tends to overrate three types of pitchers:

1. Pitchers who play in parks where scorers hand out more errors. Official scorers differ significantly in the frequency at which they assign errors to fielders.
2. Ground-ball pitchers, because a substantial proportion of errors occur on grounders.
3. Pitchers who aren't very good. Better pitchers often allow fewer unearned runs than bad pitchers, because good pitchers tend to find ways to get out of jams.

Since the last time you picked up an edition of this book, we've also made a few minor changes to DRA to make it better. Recent research into "tunneling"–the act of throwing consecutive pitches that appear similar from a batter's point of view until after the swing decision point–data has given us a new contextual factor to account for in DRA: plate distance. This refers to the distance between successive pitches as they approach the plate, and while it has a smaller effect than factors like velocity or whiff rate, it still can help explain pitcher strikeout rate in our model.

New Pitching Metrics for 2019

We're including a few "new" pitching metrics for 2019's suite of Baseball Prospectus publications, but you may be familiar with them if you've spent time scouring the internet for stats.

Fastball Percentage

Our fastball percentage (FB%) statistic measures how frequently a pitcher throws a pitch classified as a "fastball," measured as a percentage of overall pitches thrown. We qualify three types of fastballs:

1. The traditional four-seam fastball;
2. The two-seam fastball or sinker;
3. "Hard cutters," which are pitches that have the movement profile of a cut fastball and are used as the pitcher's primary offering or in place of a more traditional fastball.

For example, a pitcher with a FB% of 67 throws any combination of these three pitches about two-thirds of the time.

Whiff Rate

Everybody loves a swing and a miss, and whiff rate (WHF) measures how frequently pitchers induce a swinging strike. To calculate WHF, we add up all the pitches thrown that ended with a swinging strike, then divide that number by a pitcher's total pitches thrown. Most often, high whiff rates correlate with high strikeout rates (and overall effective pitcher performance).

Called Strike Probability

Called Strike Probability (CSP) is a number that represents the likelihood that all of a pitcher's pitches will be called a strike while controlling for location, pitcher and batter handedness, umpire and count. Here's how it works: on each pitch, our model determines how many times (out of 100) that a similar pitch was called for a strike given those factors mentioned above, and when normalized for each batter's strike zone. Then we average the CSP for all pitches thrown by a pitcher in a season, and that gives us the yearly CSP percentage you see in the stats boxes.

As you might imagine, pitchers with a higher CSP are more likely to work in the zone, where pitchers with a lower CSP are likely locating their pitches outside the normal strike zone, for better or for worse.

Projections

Many of you aren't turning to this book just for a look at what a player has done, but for a look at what a player is going to do: the PECOTA projections. PECOTA, initially developed by Nate Silver (who has moved on to greater fame as a political analyst), consists of three parts:

1. Major-league equivalencies, which use minor-league statistics to project how a player will perform in the major leagues;
2. Baseline forecasts, which use weighted averages and regression to the mean to estimate a player's current true talent level; and
3. Aging curves, which uses the career paths of comparable players to estimate how a player's statistics are likely to change over time.

With all those important things covered, let's take a look at what's in the book this year.

Team Prospectus

You bought this book to learn more about your favorite (or maybe least-favorite, who are we to judge?) team, so let's talk about them. After a thoughtful preview of the 2019 season, you'll be presented with our Team Prospectus. This outlines many of the key statistics for each team's 2018 season, as well as a very inviting stadium diagram.

First you'll find the Performance Graphs page. The first is the 2018 Hit List Ranking. This shows our Hit List Rank for the team on each day of the 2018 season and is intended to give you a picture of the ups and downs of the team's season, including their highest and lowest ranks of the year. Hit List Rank measures overall team performance and drives the Hit List Power Rankings at the baseballprospectus.com website.

The second graph is Committed Payroll and helps you see how the team's payroll has compared to the MLB and divisional average payrolls over time. Payroll figures are currents as of January 1, 2019; with so many free agents still unsigned as of this writing, the final 2018 figure will likely be significantly different for many teams. (In the meantime, you can always find the most current data at Baseball Prospectus' Cot's Baseball Contracts page.)

Arizona Diamondbacks 2019

The third graph is Farm System Ranking and displays how the Baseball Prospectus prospect team has ranked the organization's farm system since 2007. It also indicates the highest and lowest ranks that the farm system achieved over that time.

We start the Team Performance page with the squad's unadjusted and third-order 2018 win-loss records, presented in divisional context. We then list the three highest performing hitters and pitchers by WARP for 2018. Beneath that are a host of other team statistics. **Pythag** presents an adjusted 2018 winning percentage, calculated by taking runs scored per game (**RS/G**) and runs allowed per game (**RA/G**) for the team, and running them through a version of Bill James' Pythagorean formula that was refined and improved by David Smyth and Brandon Heipp. (The formula is called "Pythagenpat," which is equally fun to type and to say.)

Next up is **DRC+**, described earlier, to indicate the overall hitting ability of the team either above or below league-average. Run prevention on the pitching side is covered by **DRA** (also mentioned earlier) and another metric: Fielding Independent Pitching (**FIP**), which calculates another ERA-like statistic based on strikeouts, walks, and home runs recorded. Defensive Efficiency Rating (**DER**) tells us the percentage of balls in play turned into outs for the team, and is a quick fielding shorthand that rounds out run prevention.

After that, we have several measures related to roster composition, as opposed to on-field performance. **B-Age** and **P-Age** tell us the average age of a team's batters and pitchers, respectively. **Salary** is the combined team payroll for all on-field players, and Doug Pappas' Marginal Dollars per Marginal Win (**M$/MW**) tells us how much money a team spent to earn production above replacement level.

Ending this batch of statistics is the number of disabled list days a team had over the season (**DL Days**) and the amount of salary paid to players on the disabled list (**$ on DL**); this final number is expressed as a percentage of total payroll.

Next to each of these stats, we've listed each team's MLB rank in that category from 1st to 30th. In this, 1st always indicates a positive outcome and 30th a negative outcome, except in the case of salary–1st is highest.

The Team Projections page is intended to convey the team's operational capacity entering the 2019 season. We start with the team's PECOTA projected record for 2019, again in divisional context. The **+/-** column indicates how many more or less wins the team is projected to get than they got in 2018. We then list the three highest projected hitters and pitchers by WARP for 2018. A brief farm system summary follows, with the team's top prospect and number of BP Top 101 Prospects. Finally, we list the key new players and departed players, along with their 2019 projected WARP.

Alex Bregman 3B

Born: 03/30/94 Age: 25 Bats: R Throws: R
Height: 6'0" Weight: 180 Origin: Round 1, 2015 Draft (#2 overall)

YEAR	TEAM	LVL	AGE	PA	R	2B	3B	HR	RBI	BB	K	SB	CS	AVG/OBP/SLG
2016	CCH	AA	22	285	54	16	2	14	46	42	26	5	3	.297/.415/.559
2016	FRE	AAA	22	83	17	6	0	6	15	5	12	2	1	.333/.373/.641
2016	HOU	MLB	22	217	31	13	3	8	34	15	52	2	0	.264/.313/.478
2017	HOU	MLB	23	626	88	39	5	19	71	55	97	17	5	.284/.352/.475
2018	HOU	MLB	24	705	105	51	1	31	103	96	85	10	4	.286/.394/.532
2019	*HOU*	*MLB*	*25*	*675*	*96*	*38*	*3*	*23*	*78*	*73*	*107*	*12*	*4*	*.272/.359/.463*

Breakout: 6% Improve: 52% Collapse: 5% Attrition: 2% MLB: 100%
Comparables: Anthony Rendon, David Wright, Pablo Sandoval

YEAR	TEAM	LVL	AGE	PA	DRC+	VORP	BABIP	BRR	FRAA	WARP
2016	CCH	AA	22	285	172	38.9	.286	1.6	SS(51): -3.4, 3B(11): 1.4	2.7
2016	FRE	AAA	22	83	161	10.0	.333	-1.2	SS(14): 2.1, LF(3): -0.1	0.8
2016	HOU	MLB	22	217	107	9.6	.317	0.5	3B(40): 0.9, SS(6): -0.1	1.1
2017	HOU	MLB	23	626	114	34.7	.311	-1.5	3B(132): 8.7, SS(30): -2.9	3.9
2018	HOU	MLB	24	705	150	72.6	.289	-1.6	3B(136): 5.4, SS(28): -0.4	7.4
2019	*HOU*	*MLB*	*25*	*675*	*125*	*37.3*	*.295*	*0.0*	*3B 7, SS 0*	*4.6*

After the projections page, we share a few items about the team's home ballpark. There's the aforementioned diagram of the park's dimensions (including distances to the outfield wall), a few important biographical facts about the stadium, a graphic showing the height of the wall from the left-field pole to the right-field pole, and a table showing three-year park factors for the stadium. The park factors are displayed as indexes where 100 is average, 110 means that the park inflates the statistic in question by 10 percent, and 90 means that the park deflates the statistic in question by 10 percent.

Following the ballpark page, we have a **Personnel** section that lists many of the important decision-makers and upper-level field and operations staff members for the franchise, as well as any former Baseball Prospectus staff members who are currently part of the organization.

Position Players

After all that information and a thoughtful bylined essay covering each team, we present our player comments. Each player is listed with the major-league team who employed him as of early January 2019. If a player changed teams after that point via free agency, trade, or any other method, you'll be able to find them in the book for their previous squad.

First, we cover biographical information (age is as of June 30, 2019) before moving onto the stats themselves. Our statistic columns include standard identifying information like **YEAR**, **TEAM**, **LVL** (level of affiliated play) and **AGE** before getting into the numbers. Next, we provide raw, unstranslated numbers like you might find on the back of your dad's baseball cards: **PA** (plate appearances), **R** (runs), **2B** (doubles), **3B** (triples), **HR** (home runs), **RBI** (runs batted in), **BB** (walks), **K** (strikeouts), **SB** (stolen bases) and **CS** (caught stealing). Then we have unadjusted "slash" statistics: **AVG** (batting average), **OBP** (on-base percentage) and **SLG** (slugging percentage).

Just below the stats box is **PECOTA** data, which is discussed further in a following section. After that, it's on to a pithy and always-informative comment written by a member of the Baseball Prospectus staff, before we cover more stats.

The second text box repeats YEAR, TEAM, LVL, AGE, and PA, then moves on to **DRC+** (Deserved Runs Created Plus), which we described earlier as total offensive expected contribution compared to the league average. Next, one of our oldest active metrics, **VORP** (Value Over Replacement Player), considers offensive production, position and plate appearances. In essence, it is the number of runs contributed beyond what a replacement-level player at the same position would contribute if given the same percentage of team plate appearances. VORP does not consider the quality of a player's defense.

BABIP (batting average on balls in play) tells us how often a ball in play fell for a hit, and can help us identify whether a batter may have been lucky or not ... but note that high BABIPs also tend to follow the great hitters of our time, as well as speedy singles hitters who put the ball on the ground.

The next item is **BRR** (Baserunning Runs), which covers all of a player's baserunning accomplishments which includes (but isn't limited to) swiped bags and failed attempts. Next is **FRAA** (Fielding Runs Above Average), which also includes the number of games previously played at each position noted in parentheses. Multi-position players have only their two most frequent positions listed here, but their total FRAA number reflects all positions played.

Our last column here is **WARP** (Wins Above Replacement Player). WARP estimates the total value of a player, which means for hitters it takes into account hitting runs above average (calculated using the DRC+ model), BRR and FRAA. Then, it makes an adjustment for positions played and gives the player a credit for plate appearances based upon the difference between "replacement level"¬–which is derived from the quality of players added to a team's roster after the start of the season¬–and the league average.

Catchers

Catchers are a special breed, and thus they have earned their own separate box which displays some of the defensive metrics that we've built just for them. As an example, let's check out J.T. Realmuto.

YEAR	TEAM	P. COUNT	FRM RUNS	BLK RUNS	THRW RUNS	TOT RUNS
2016	MIA	18935	-8.5	1.8	2.1	-5.6
2017	MIA	18959	5.3	1.7	1.0	9.1
2018	MIA	16399	-0.4	0.9	0.1	0.4
2019	PHI	18448	-1.4	1.5	0.7	0.8

The **YEAR** and **TEAM** columns match what you'd find in the other stat box. **P. COUNT** indicates the number of pitches thrown while the catcher was behind the plate, including swinging strikes, fouls, and balls in play. **FRM RUNS** is the total run value the catcher provided (or cost) his team by influencing the umpire to call strikes where other catchers did not. **BLK RUNS** expresses the total run value above or below average for the catcher's ability to prevent wild pitches and passed balls. **THRW RUNS** is calculated using a similar model as the previous two statistics, and it measures a catcher's ability to throw out basestealers but also to dissuade them from testing his arm in the first place. It takes into account factors like the pitcher (including his delivery and pickoff move) and baserunner (who could be as fast as Billy Hamilton or as slow as Yonder Alonso). **TOT RUNS** is the sum of all of the previous three statistics.

Pitchers

Let's give our pitchers a turn, using 2018 NL Cy Young winner Jacob deGrom as our example. Take a look at his first stat block: the first line and the **YEAR**, **TEAM**, **LVL** and **AGE** columns are the same as in the position player example earlier.

Here too, we have a series of columns that display raw, unadjusted statistics compiled by the pitcher over the course of a season: **W** (wins), **L** (losses), **SV** (saves), **G** (games pitched), **GS** (games started), **IP** (innings pitched), **H** (hits allowed) and **HR** (home runs allowed). Next we have two statistics that are rates: **BB/9** (walks per nine innings) and **K/9** (strikeouts per nine innings), before returning to the unadjusted **K** (strikeouts).

Next up is **GB%** (ground ball percentage), which is the percentage of all batted balls that were hit in the ground, including both outs and hits. Remember, this is based on observational data and subject to human error, so please approach this with a healthy dose of skepticism.

BABIP (batting average on balls in play) is calculated using the same methodology as it is for position players, but it often tells us more about a pitcher than it does a hitter. With pitchers, a high BABIP is often due to poor defense or bad luck, and can often be an indicator of potential rebound, and a low BABIP may be cause to expect performance regression. (A typical league-average BABIP is close to .290-.300.)

After a witty 150ish words on the player like only Baseball Prospectus's staff can provide, it's on to that second stat block, which repeats the YEAR, TEAM, LVL, and AGE columns. The metrics **WHIP** (walks plus hits per inning pitched) and **ERA**

Arizona Diamondbacks 2019

(earned run average) are old standbys: WHIP measures walks and hits allowed on a per-inning basis, while ERA measures earned runs on a nine-inning basis. Neither of these stats are translated or adjusted.

DRA (Deserved Run Average) was described at length earlier, and measures how many runs the pitcher "deserved" to allow per nine innings. Please note that since we lack all the data points that would make for a "real" DRA for minor-league events, the DRA displayed for minor league partial-seasons is based off of different data. (That data is a modified version of our cFIP metric, which you can find more information about on our website.)

Jacob deGrom   RHP

Born: 06/19/88   Age: 31   Bats: L   Throws: R
Height: 6'4"   Weight: 180   Origin: Round 9, 2010 Draft (#272 overall)

YEAR	TEAM	LVL	AGE	W	L	SV	G	GS	IP	H	HR	BB/9	K/9	K	GB%	BABIP
2016	NYN	MLB	28	7	8	0	24	24	148	142	15	2.2	8.7	143	47%	.312
2017	NYN	MLB	29	15	10	0	31	31	201[1]	180	28	2.6	10.7	239	48%	.305
2018	NYN	MLB	30	10	9	0	32	32	217	152	10	1.9	11.2	269	48%	.281
2019	NYN	MLB	31	13	9	0	31	31	186	145	18	2.3	10.7	221	46%	.286

Breakout: 8%   Improve: 29%   Collapse: 28%   Attrition: 6%   MLB: 85%
Comparables: Erik Bedard, A.J. Burnett, CC Sabathia

YEAR	TEAM	LVL	AGE	WHIP	ERA	DRA	WARP	MPH	FB%	WHF	CSP
2016	NYN	MLB	28	1.20	3.04	3.30	3.5	96.3	59.6	12.1	47.2
2017	NYN	MLB	29	1.19	3.53	3.02	5.7	97.2	55.5	14.5	49.5
2018	NYN	MLB	30	0.91	1.70	2.09	8.0	98.2	52.1	16.3	48.4
2019	NYN	MLB	31	1.02	2.91	3.23	3.9	96.6	54.5	14.8	48.2

Just like with hitters, **WARP** (Wins Above Replacement Player) is a total value metric that puts pitchers of all stripes on the same scale as position players. We use DRA as the primary input for our calculation of WARP. You might notice that relief pitchers (due to their limited innings) may have a lower WARP than you were expecting or than you might see in other WARP-like metrics. WARP does not take leverage into account, just the actions a pitcher performs and the expected value of those actions ... which ends up judging high-leverage relief pitchers differently than you might imagine given their prestige and market value.

MPH gives you the pitcher's 95th percentile velocity for the noted season, in order to give you an idea of what the *peak* fastball velocity a pitcher possesses. Since this comes from our pitch tracking data, it is not publicly available for minor-league pitchers.

Finally, we display the three new pitching metrics we described earlier. **FB%** (fastball percentage) gives you the percentage of fastballs thrown out of all pitches. **WhiffRt** (whiff rate) tells you the percentage of swinging strikes induced out of all pitches. **CS Prob** (called strike probability) expresses the likelihood of all pitches thrown to result in a called strike, after controlling for factors like handedness, umpire, pitch type, count, and location.

PECOTA

All players have PECOTA projections for 2019, as well as a set of other numbers that describe the performance of comparable players according to PECOTA. All projections for 2019 are for the player at the date we went to press in early January and are projected into the league and park context as indicated by the team abbreviation. All PECOTA projected statistics represent a player's projected major-league performance.

The numbers beneath the player's stats–Breakout, Improve, Collapse, Attrition–are part and parcel of the PECOTA projections. They estimate the likelihood of changes in performance relative to the player's previously-established level of production, based on the performance of comparable players:

Breakout Rate is the percent change that a player's production will improve by at least 20 percent relative to the weighted average of his performance over his most recent seasons.

Improve Rate is the percent chance that a player's production will improve at all relative to his baseline performance. A player who is expected to perform just the same as he has in the recent past will have an Improve Rate of 50 percent.

Collapse Rate is the percent chance that a position player's production will decline by at least 25 percent relative to his baseline performance.

Attrition Rate operates on playing time rather than performance. Specifically, it measures the likelihood that a player's playing time will decrease by at least 50 percent relative to his established level.

Breakout Rate and Collapse Rate can sometimes be counterintuitive for players who have already experienced a radical change in performance level. It's also worth noting that the projected decline in a player's rate performances might not be indicative of an expected decline in underlying ability or skill, but could just be an anticipated correction following a breakout season.

MLB% is the percentage of similar players who played in the major leagues in their relevant season.

The final pieces of information are the player's three highest-scoring comparable players as determined by PECOTA. All comparables represent a snapshot of how the listed player was performing at the same age as the current player, so if a 23-year-old pitcher is compared to Bartolo Colon, he's actually being compared to a 23-year-old Colon, not the version that pitched for the Rangers in 2018, nor to Colon's career as a whole.

Arizona Diamondbacks 2019

A few points about pitcher projections. First, we aren't yet projecting peak velocity, so that column will be blank in the PECOTA lines. Second, projecting DRA is trickier than evaluating past performance, because it is unclear how deserving each pitcher will be of his anticipated outcomes. However, we know that another DRA-related statistic–contextual FIP or cFIP–estimates future run scoring very well. So for PECOTA, the projected DRA figures you see are based on the past cFIPs generated by the pitcher and comparable players over time, along with the other factors described above.

Lineouts

In each chapter's Lineouts section, you'll find abbreviated text comments, as well as most of same information you'd find in our full player comments. We limit the stats boxes in this section to only including the 2018 information for each player.

Exclusive Player Visualizations

In our constant battle to provide you with new and interesting baseball content you can't find anywhere else, we've added a trio of data visualizations to each hitter's entry in these books and a pair of visualizations for each pitcher.

For hitters, you'll find three new infographics. The first is each player's **Batted Ball Distribution**, which displays the five major sections of the field: LF (left), LCF (left center), CF (center), RCF (right center), and RF (right). The percentage indicated tells us what percentage of batted balls from that hitter fell within that part of the field during the 2018 season. We've also included the hitter's slugging percentage on balls in play (also called **SLGCON**) for that part of the field.

You'll also see two heatmaps: **Strike Zone vs LHP** and **Strike Zone vs RHP**. These heat maps represent a view of the strike zone from behind the catcher. Areas where there is a darker coloration represent the places where a higher percentage of pitches resulted in hits. In other words, the heatmap represents a hitter's "sweet spots" for getting hits against either left-handed or right-handed pitchers, depending on the image.

Pitchers get two images that help explain what their pitches look like from a hitter's perspective: **Pitch Shape vs LHH** and **Pitch Shape vs RHH**. These images show you the shape and the "tunneling" effect of each pitcher's offerings from the batter's perspective. For each type of pitch that a pitcher throws (represented by an indicator shape), there's a set of dots indicating the flight path, where each dot represents a 0.01-second interval. This maps the average trajectory and speed of an offering, ending where the ball crosses the plate. The solid black box represents the regular strike zone, while the gray contour lines indicate the range of locations that a pitcher typically works in.

Below the image, we provide a bit more detailed information about each pitcher's average offering in the **Pitch Types** box. Here, we also list each of the pitcher's major offerings under the **Type** column.

- **Fastballs** (which usually refers to the four-seam variation)
- **Sinkers** and/or two-seam fastballs
- **Cutters** (which could include "hard" cutters like cut fastballs and "soft" cutters that resemble hard sliders)
- **Changeups** (not including most splitters)
- **Splitters** (split-fingered pitches, forkballs, and some split-changes)
- **Sliders** and/or slurves
- **Curveballs** (including spike-curveballs and knuckle-curveballs, as well as some slurvy curves)
- **Slow curveballs** and/or eephus pitches
- **Knuckleballs**
- **Screwballs**

The **Freq** column indicates the percentage of overall pitches that fall into each of those type categories; if a pitcher has a 16.55% score for changeups, then that's the percent of all pitches that he throws as changeups. **Velo** is exactly what you think it is: the average miles per hour for each pitch type. **H Mov** is the number of inches of horizontal movement on the average pitch of that type, while **V Mov** is the number of inches of vertical movement on the average pitch of that type. (At Baseball Prospectus, we measure this over the long flight of the ball and include gravity into the V Mov number in order to give you the most realistic representation of what the pitch *actually* does.)

If you're wondering about the second number in brackets, that's the index for that velocity or movement compared to the league average. Like DRC+, a score of 100 means that the speed or movement is about the same as league average, while a higher score means that there's higher velocity or movement than the league average. Numbers below 100 indicate less velocity or movement than the league average.

Part 1: Team Analysis

Table for Two: Previewing the 2019 Arizona Diamondbacks

Randy Holt and Jeff Wiser

JEFF WISER: It's going to be really hard to have this conversation without acknowledging the elephant in the room, so let's just get to it. A.J. Pollock and Patrick Corbin walked in free agency. Paul Goldschmidt was traded. One could easily argue that the trio represented three of the four best players from last year's team. How did the Diamondbacks do this winter?

RANDY HOLT: I, uh, yeah. It seems like everything the front office did was a tough look for what very well should have been a strong contender last season. I get letting guys like Pollock and Corbin walk, because their skill sets are ultimately replaceable, on some level, relative to the amount of money they were set to make. But trading your all-world face of the franchise? Yeah, free agency on the horizon, etc., but why not just a full-scale teardown at that point? They're stuck in this weird hellish, purgatory-type middle ground that isn't really interesting for anybody involved, save for a few individual younger guys.

JEFF: You're spot-on: it's a strange tactic to shoot for the middle again and hope for a better outcome. On the one hand, I think we've been conditioned a bit recently to think you have to either be pushing in or selling hard (i.e. "tanking"). So maybe there's some value to zigging while the others zag. With several sellers active in the early offseason, maybe the trade returns just weren't there. But on the other hand, having a roster full of adequate players that aren't exactly "great" is purgatorial. This team flirted with this scenario a couple of years ago and it didn't work out too well.

I suppose they got some good pieces in return from the Goldy deal and the draft picks for letting Corbin and Pollock walk have their own value. I, personally, don't have a huge problem with any of it, although it'll be super strange to see Goldschmidt wearing #46 and a sharper shade of red. The draft side of it is really intriguing to me. They're going to have a massive bonus pool to work with this summer and the early indications are that this class is full of bats, particularly college-aged ones—something they still need to add. While the payoff isn't until June, the groundwork was technically laid this offseason and that's a win, even if it won't be evident for quite some time.

But back to the guys who will be on the field this year. They really need a player or two that will do the heavy lifting. Is there anyone you have in mind that can take that role and run with it?

RANDY: They have a lot of guys who I feel are great supplementary pieces, but nobody who can be "that dude", in my opinion. David Peralta has posted a couple of really strong years, with identical looks in the AVG and OBP departments (.293 and .352, respectively) in 2017-2018, but PECOTA really doesn't like him this year. It has his average dipping by nearly 30 points and his DRC+ falling all the way down to 102, a far cry from his 125 mark of last year.

I like Ketel Marte a lot, but he's a streaky guy who I don't think is capable of carrying an offense. Eduardo Escobar is a really solid piece, but not exactly a huge boon for the offense. Steven Souza? Coming off a 30 homer campaign, his season was obviously ravaged by injury, but PECOTA isn't terribly in favor of a rebound there, with a DRC+ coming in at an even 100. And look, everyone knows I stan Jake Lamb like no other, but he has to stay healthy. He's probably the biggest source of power on the roster, but this is a guy who has either missed significant time or had injury limit his production severely. So, to answer your question, I don't think there really is *that guy*. If I *had* to choose, I go Peralta, but the options here aren't terribly encouraging.

JEFF: See, this underscores what you said before about the "middle." All of those guys are capable of being league-average of slightly better than that. The good news is that there aren't any total black holes. The bad news is that it's still not enough and the team just isn't going to spend wildly at this point for marginal upgrades (though you could certainly argue that they should). The Diamondbacks seem like they're one impact bat short of really pushing into the positive when it comes to offensive production. You know, they could really use Paul Goldsh…

I suppose if I have to really find a player who just might lead the way, perhaps unexpectedly, I'll go with Steven Souza. Look, the pectoral injuries derailed his 2018 season before it really started and he just never got back on track after that. He missed time with multiple DL stints and appeared to do something differently with his approach, but started to get back to his old ways in the last few weeks of the season. There's still plenty of raw to work with, and yeah he strikes out, but he'll walk at a strong clip and get on base where he can actually steal a bag or two. I don't know if he's a "carry the offense guy," but I think he's going to be significantly better than what most people expect.

On the pitching side, I'm just going to go ahead and state it now: Robbie Ray is going to have a huge year. He was strong down the stretch last season after missing time to injury earlier in his campaign. Ray still walked too many dudes (5.09 BB/9), but he was back to his ways of just keeping the ball out of play (batters hit just .215 against him) and sending guys back to the dugout empty-handed (12.01 K/9). He's my real-deal, pick-to-click, "breakout" player on this roster. The tools are there and he's done it before. Lock it in for me.

RANDY: You're a braver man than I with your declarations. I'm still recovering from being burned by my being really eager and sure of Shelby Miller's inevitable return to form to maintain that kind of confidence in anything. As such, let's talk about somebody we're down on. I feel like Nick Ahmed is an easy answer, because I think he should just be better than what he is. But you know how it is with defense. So instead I'll look at the pitching side with my birthday twin Zack Godley. Like many, I was relatively high on him heading into 2018 coming off a big year, with that 3.37 ERA and 1.14 WHIP. But he regressed in just about every way. His walks were up, his velocity was down, and he gave up a startling amount of hard contact. I still feel like he wasn't completely healthy, but he doesn't have the arsenal in terms of velocity and movement to lack command like he did. PECOTA likes a return to form, but I just don't see it.

JEFF: That's a fair point, and I think when PECOTA does swing and miss, there's usually something going on behind the scenes that it just can't account for. In this case, his mechanics have been sloppy at times with him falling off the mound like a scoop of ice cream off a cone in 110-degree heat.

I'll go another direction: Wilmer Flores. Maybe it's not fair to pick on the new guy, but I just think his signing was way out of character for the organization and that's going to put him in a tough spot. Look, he's another slightly better than league average hitter—but he's not a second baseman anymore. At least not for something approaching 125 games. His knees are about as up to that challenge as mine are. And if he struggles there defensively but keeps getting run out to the keystone, does that lead to any trouble at the dish?

RANDY: Yeah, I think the signing itself kind of fits the mold of middle-of-the-road level of achievement that the Diamondbacks are clearly striving for here. Also, can I make a comment about Zack Godley sweating like a melting ice cream cone by the end of the first inning, just to further your point there?

JEFF: Haha! Yes, he is a big-time pitcher on occasion, but always a big-time persperator. On a serious note, he is a real hardass on the mound and competes his tail off. The team if full of these kinds of guys—players that really try as hard as they can. And in that way, I do think this team will give good effort. Torey Lovullo is a great communicator and seems to understand how to get the most of his guys. At the end of the day, I just wonder what that's all worth. It's a nice narrative and is a great sign longer-term, but how much does it matter in the here and now? The latest PECOTA update gives them an 82-80 record. How does this whole thing end up?

RANDY: I don't think that PECOTA is too far off here. They're definitely as easy to identify as a .500 squad as there is in baseball. Their upside was probably higher than what the actual end result was last year. There are some offensive pieces, like we talked about, and I think if those pieces come together, they'll excel. But those pieces have also been prone to bouts of streakiness, if you will. Like last May when literally the entire team forgot how to hit. I think the pitching staff could fare much the same. Up at times, but not quite "up" enough to compensate for the down they'll experience. Like you said, they've got a really strong presence at the end of the dugout there so it's going to be really interesting to see what he can do with what is very much a mid-tier squad.

JEFF: It feels like a .500 record is appropriate for the talent level of the team. They have few, if any, black holes but also very few, if any, dominant performers. That's essentially the definition of a .500 ballclub. But baseball just rarely plays out that way. If the Diamondbacks find themselves in the hunt come midseason, they could add a piece or two and take advantage of teams who decide to throw in the towel, pushing past the 82-win mark by a few. But on the flip side, if they have a key injury or just fall out of contention early, I could see Mike Hazen cashing in some more pieces at the deadline. David Peralta, Nick Ahmed, Robbie Ray, maybe even Zack Greinke could draw interest near the trade deadline. And if that's how it goes, since they could be closer to 72 wins than 82 wins. So for me, it's one of those scenarios at the end of the day—an impressive win total at the end of the year or a disappointing one capped off with a few key trades. The Diamondbacks are probably a .500 team from a talent perspective, but I think the end result goes differently. In which direction is very much to be determined.

Performance Graphs

2018 Hit List Ranking

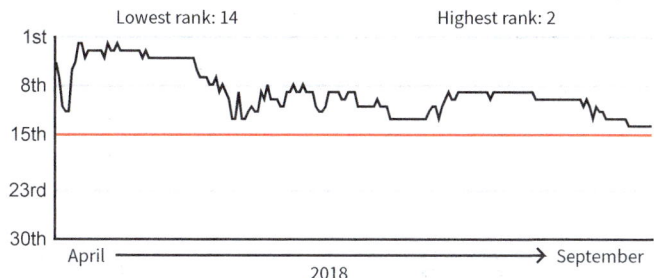

Committed Payroll (in millions)

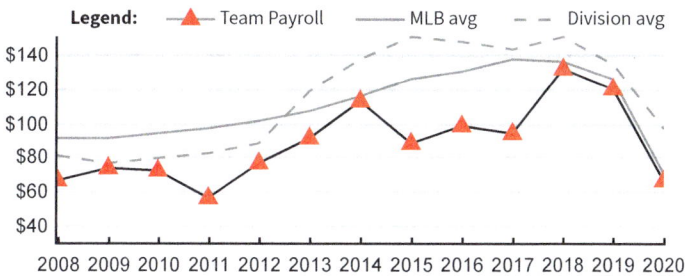

Farm System Ranking

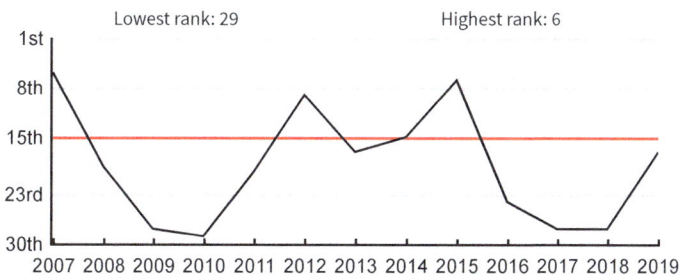

2018 Team Performance

ACTUAL STANDINGS

Team	W	L	Pct
LAN	92	71	.564
COL	91	72	.558
ARI	**82**	**80**	**.506**
SFN	73	89	.450
SDN	66	96	.407

THIRD-ORDER STANDINGS

Team	W	L	Pct
LAN	105	58	.644
COL	88	75	.539
ARI	**87**	**75**	**.537**
SFN	71	91	.438
SDN	66	96	.407

TOP HITTERS

Player	WARP
Paul Goldschmidt	4.1
Nick Ahmed	3.3
Ketel Marte	2.9

TOP PITCHERS

Player	WARP
Patrick Corbin	5.9
Zack Greinke	5.3
Robbie Ray	1.9

VITAL STATISTICS

Statistic Name	Value	Rank
Pythagenpat	.534	13th
Runs Scored per Game	4.28	20th
Runs Allowed per Game	3.98	4th
Deserved Runs Created Plus	89	26th
Deserved Run Average	4.21	11th
Fielding Independent Pitching	3.87	8th
Defensive Efficiency Rating	.711	9th
Batter Age	29.2	26th
Pitcher Age	29.6	26th
Salary	$131.6M	17th
Marginal $ per Marginal Win	$3.5M	20th
Disabled List Days	$945.0M	10th
$ on DL	14%	11th

2019 Team Projections

PROJECTED STANDINGS

Team	W	L	Pct	+/-
LAN	93	69	.574	+1
COL	84	78	.518	-7
ARI	**81**	**81**	**.500**	**-1**
SDN	79	83	.487	+13
SFN	73	89	.450	0

TOP PROJECTED HITTERS

Player	WARP
Wilmer Flores	2.1
Ketel Marte	2.0
Nick Ahmed	2.0

TOP PROJECTED PITCHERS

Player	WARP
Robbie Ray	2.4
Zack Greinke	2.4
Zack Godley	2.0

FARM SYSTEM REPORT

Top Prospect	Number of Top 101 Prospects
Jazz Chisholm, #69	3

KEY DEDUCTIONS

Player	WARP
Paul Goldschmidt	5.4
Patrick Corbin	3.3
Jeff Mathis	2.0
A.J. Pollock	1.9
Shelby Miller	1.4
Chris Owings	0.6
Brad Boxberger	0.5
Jon Jay	0.4
Jake Diekman	0.4
Daniel Descalso	0.3
Clay Buchholz	0.3

KEY ADDITIONS

Player	WARP
Wilmer Flores	2.1
Adam Jones	2
Carson Kelly	1.5
Luke Weaver	1.3

Team Personnel

President
Derrick Hall

Executive VP, General Manager
Mike Hazen

Senior Vice President, Assistant GM
Amiel Sawdaye

Senior Vice President, Assistant GM
Jared Porter

Manager
Torey Lovullo

BP Alumni
Hudson Belinsky
Tucker Blair
Jason Parks

Chase Field Stats

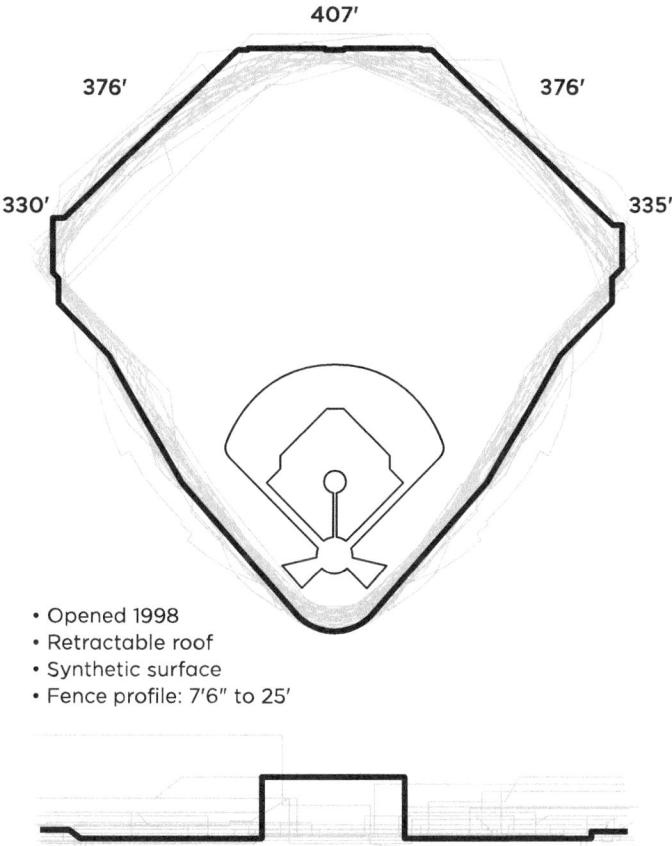

- Opened 1998
- Retractable roof
- Synthetic surface
- Fence profile: 7'6" to 25'

Three-Year Park Factors

Runs	Runs/RH	Runs/LH	HR/RH	HR/LH
107	108	106	108	102

Diamondbacks Team Analysis

Diamondbacks closer Brad Boxberger had a 2.89 ERA, 24 saves in 28 tries and 52 strikeouts in 37 1/3 innings through July 24 of last season. Arizona was 56-46, just a half-game behind the Dodgers for first place in the NL West, and Boxberger was mowing batters down with his straightforward fastball-changeup mix despite that heater working much more at 91-92 miles per hour than at 93-94. The Diamondbacks had dealt for him on the eve of the non-tender deadline in November 2017, when the Rays were poised to cut him loose and in no position to demand anything meaningful in return. Now, it appeared, Arizona had shored up his shortcomings well enough to turn him back into the relief ace-caliber righty he'd been in 2014 and 2015.

On July 26, however, Boxberger gave up back-to-back homers to David Bote and Anthony Rizzo of the Cubs, blowing a two-run lead and sending the Diamondbacks to a walk-off loss on a getaway day in Chicago. Astutely sensing trouble (and needing to act on the lack of depth around Boxberger and setup man Archie Bradley, anyway), executive vice president and general manager Mike Hazen and the rest of the front office made two deals on the day of the trade deadline to bolster the bullpen, adding left-hander Jake Diekman and right-hander Brad Ziegler to the relief corps.

It worked, briefly, largely thanks to the jolt of another deadline acquisition, switch-hitting infielder Eduardo Escobar. Between August 25 and September 9, however, Boxberger blew (or aided in blowing) four more games, as the team began to spiral downward. Boxberger had a 7.88 ERA over his final 20 appearances, surrendering a .297/.418/.516 batting line. The Diamondbacks finished 8-19 in September, a fitting way to tumble from contention for a club plagued by inconsistency. They were utterly Jekyll and Hyde: 20-8 at the end of April, 8-19 in May, 19-9 in June. Boxberger was a microcosm of the team: surprising, impressive, then, when it mattered most, unable to come through.

As much as Boxberger embodied the Diamondbacks last season, the Diamondbacks also embody what it is to follow a baseball team right now. There's endless promise. There's always something by which to be impressed. Ultimately, though, there is inevitable frustration, and not in an only-one-team-can-win-the-championship kind of way, but in a troublesome, anti-competitive sense. Picking up Boxberger for pennies on the dollar was a neat trick, but if the Diamondbacks hadn't been engaged in careful shoestring budgeting, they never would have needed to rely on Boxberger the way they did. They could still have had him, but they could have had him in a lower-leverage role, surrounded by other, superior bullpen options.

That frustration only mounts now, as the team moves into a new phase without the two best homegrown players they've ever developed, Paul Goldschmidt and Patrick Corbin. The $131 million payroll the Diamondbacks ran in 2018 was a franchise record, by nearly $20 million, and owner Ken Kendrick viewed it as untenable. The team has paid more than $100 million for its MLB roster just three times in its history, and just twice since 2004, when Kendrick and his minority partners took over. It was no surprise when the marching orders came down and the baseball operations department was forced to find the best deal it could for Goldschmidt, owed $14.5 million in his final season before free agency, but that's only because baseball owners have so thoroughly accustomed their fans to view the situation through a distorted lens.

In late 2012, MLB rounded out its national television rights package for a total of $4.2 billion through 2021, an average annual per-team payout of more than $40 million. In February 2015, the Diamondbacks and FOX agreed to a 15-year local TV rights deal worth over $1.5 billion, which works out to $100 million or more per season. In early 2018, every MLB team received a one-time payment of $50 million for their share of the stake in MLB Advanced Media that the league sold to Disney. In November 2018, FOX extended its national TV rights deal with MLB for $5.1 billion through 2028, locking in a rate hike of more than 20 percent. Without selling a single ticket, Kendrick and company could pay that team-high payroll from 2018 every season from 2019 through at least 2030, even if that $50 million check went straight into their pockets and never came out.

Zack Greinke's contract provided unfortunate cover for Diamondbacks ownership, just as similar big-money free agent signings have done similar things for owners throughout the game. Greinke had his worst season since 2007 in the first year of that six-year, $206 million pact, and Kendrick and chief executive officer Derrick Hall fired general manager Dave Stewart at the end of that 2016 season. Shortly after that, a new Collective Bargaining Agreement was finalized, introducing harsher penalties for spending beyond the luxury-tax threshold and restrictions on various forms of amateur talent acquisition. All of which led to the team being able to encourage the development of a local narrative within the Phoenix sports scene, absolving them of further responsibility to spend aggressively and laying the blame for their potential inability to get over the hump at the feet of a Hall of Fame-caliber pitcher.

It also gave the Diamondbacks added leverage in an ongoing dispute with Maricopa County about the costs of repairs and upgrades to Chase Field. In May 2018, the Diamondbacks essentially won that legal dispute. They gained control of funding allocation for stadium maintenance, increasing their leeway to spend those funds on non-structural things like a new scoreboard and improved air conditioning, and they secured the right to explore leaving Chase Field for a new stadium elsewhere in the Phoenix area five years earlier than their lease had otherwise allowed.

No thread should tie a big free agent deal to those kinds of negotiations, nor to high-level team strategy in a league as universally profitable as MLB is. However, because the owners have beaten the players as consistently in the court of public opinion as at the bargaining table, the partitions that ought to separate business decisions from baseball decisions have all but disappeared. Teams have no problem whatsoever selling cynical financial choices to their fan bases as on-field choices merely focused on long-term competitiveness and analytics.

Here enters Hazen and his troupe of erstwhile Theo Epstein and Ben Cherington disciples. They're among the best and fastest-improving front offices in baseball, having not only established a respected top-level brain trust, but cobbled together one of the more quietly effective and comprehensive baseball operations shops in the game. In 2016, under Stewart Diamondbacks catchers ranked 25th in Adjusted Fielding Runs Above, BP's defensive metric that bakes in pitch framing and pitch blocking as well as throwing and fielding. In 2017, after Hazen's crew signed veteran Jeff Mathis to anchor the catching unit, the team was eighth-best in Adjusted FRAA. In 2018, they were the best in baseball—edging out the Dodgers, who had led MLB in that category for two straight seasons.

It wasn't just about the front office's willingness to accept Mathis's poor offense as a tradeoff to carry his great glove, either. The on-field coaching staff, with help from the analytics department, also materially improved the pitch-framing performances of Chris Iannetta and Alex Avila during those two seasons. To help players improve in crucial, undervalued skills like framing is a very valuable organizational skill, and framing isn't the only area where Arizona has demonstrated it.

After a few of their players (A.J. Pollock, Chris Owings, Mitch Haniger) began to buy heavily into the air-ball revolution just before Stewart's departure, the new front office encouraged the same kinds of changes from other hitters in 2017, and redoubled their commitment to that approach in 2018 by hiring Robert Van Scoyoc as a hitting strategist, a non-coaching role in which he nonetheless provided frequent input and helped the team get the most out of the talent on hand. Consider Daniel Descalso. At age 31 and in his second year with the Diamondbacks, previously light-hitting utility man Descalso had by far the best season of his career, posting a .789 OPS and a 110 DRC+ in 423 plate appearances.

During the two previous seasons, Descalso had radically adjusted his approach, becoming far more selective and (thereby) boosting his on-base percentage. With the help of Van Scoyoc and Diamondbacks hitting coaches Dave Magadan and Tim Laker, he took his transformation a step farther. Swinging a bit more often but much more aggressively, Descalso brought his ground-ball rate down from just under 39 percent to under 31 percent—the sixth-lowest figure in MLB among all hitters with at least 300 plate appearances. He pulled the ball more and hit it harder. Though still not an elite power hitter, Descalso began generating enough pop to make his still-patient approach play up.

All over the roster, in every aspect of the game, the new front office made significant investments and demonstrated a nimble progressiveness typical of the Red Sox and Cubs organizations from which so many of them came. They've employed former pitcher Dan Haren as a pitching strategist, a role similar to that of Van Scoyoc (who has since been hired as the Dodgers' hitting coach). Through Haren's and other influences, the team has drawn impressive improvements out of talented pitchers like Patrick Corbin, Robbie Ray, Taijuan Walker and Archie Bradley.

They traded Haniger and shortstop Jean Segura for Walker and Ketel Marte, and turned Marte into both a more productive hitter and a vital piece of the National League's best defensive infield. They won 93 games in 2017 and 82 (with a third-order record of 87-75) in 2018, without damaging their farm system. They might even have strengthened it, despite their trade for J.D. Martinez in July 2017. This is what an exceptionally talented front office with a deep staff can accomplish, even during an era in which almost every front office is smarter than any front office was 20 years ago.

Yet, there that front office was, in early December, reluctantly dealing away its cornerstone, Goldschmidt, days after letting its co-ace, Corbin, sign elsewhere. They made a fine deal with the Cardinals, one very much in line with the points of strength and emphasis within the front office. They got a young, valuable starting pitcher (Luke Weaver) who might thrive in a move to relief the way Bradley did, a catcher (Carson Kelly) who can continue their defensive excellence behind the plate and a prospect (Andy Young) who's come out of nowhere on the strength of surprising power from a small frame. They also got a draft pick, and like any group descended from House Epstein, this front office knows how to maximize the value of extra draft picks. Arizona will also receive extra picks from the free agent departures of Corbin and A.J. Pollock.

For the hardcore baseball fan, immersed in the numbers and fascinated by the minutiae of team-building, the Diamondbacks will be fun to watch over the coming year. For most fans, though, and for anyone who enjoys the game on the field more than the behind-the-scenes details of its production, they might be something of a bummer. They're unlikely to be as good as they have been over the past two seasons, not because their top talent got old or because they weren't quick enough to evolve with an ever-changing game, but because their owners would rather pocket scores (rather than tens) of millions of dollars than retain the faces of their franchise, potentially creating a vacuum of production, leadership and fan affection that won't easily be filled. This isn't unique to the

Diamondbacks. It's happening all over the league. But baseball fandom is provincial, so it's being felt only as it happens to each team, one by one. This season, it could be on display most vividly in Arizona.

—*Matthew Trueblood is an author of Baseball Prospectus.*

Part 2: Player Analysis

Arizona Diamondbacks 2019

Nick Ahmed SS
Born: 03/15/90   Age: 29   Bats: R   Throws: R
Height: 6'2"   Weight: 195   Origin: Round 2, 2011 Draft (#85 overall)

YEAR	TEAM	LVL	AGE	PA	R	2B	3B	HR	RBI	BB	K	SB	CS	AVG/OBP/SLG
2016	ARI	MLB	26	308	26	9	1	4	20	15	58	5	2	.218/.265/.299
2017	ARI	MLB	27	178	24	8	1	6	21	10	39	3	4	.251/.298/.419
2018	ARI	MLB	28	564	61	33	5	16	70	40	109	5	4	.234/.290/.411
2019	ARI	MLB	29	524	58	24	3	13	54	40	104	7	5	.241/.303/.386

Breakout: 6%   Improve: 46%   Collapse: 9%   Attrition: 23%   MLB: 90%
Comparables: Angel Berroa, Brendan Ryan, Paul Janish

For a while there, the Mendoza Line was dangerously close to being renamed. Calling it the "Hechavarria Line" was too much of a mouthful for most and the "Ahmed Line" seemed a better fit. At least until Ahmed broke his own mold by flirting with league-average offense for most of 2018. A mainstay in the lineup for his defensive chops, he finally made some headway by staying a bit more within himself at the plate. Ahmed chased less and produced more power than ever before. He nearly eclipsed his career total for home runs in just a single season and picked up some slack against right-handed pitching. He was again among the league leaders in FRAA and put together enough offense to avoid being a total black hole. It's been decided — the Hechavarria Line it is.

YEAR	TEAM	LVL	AGE	PA	DRC+	VORP	BABIP	BRR	FRAA	WARP
2016	ARI	MLB	26	308	63	-4.8	.258	2.3	SS(88): 9.4	1.2
2017	ARI	MLB	27	178	80	1.7	.295	-0.8	SS(48): 3.9	0.7
2018	ARI	MLB	28	564	89	17.1	.265	-0.4	SS(148): 15.1	3.3
2019	ARI	MLB	29	524	84	11.6	.282	-0.8	SS 10	2.0

Nick Ahmed, continued

Batted Ball Distribution

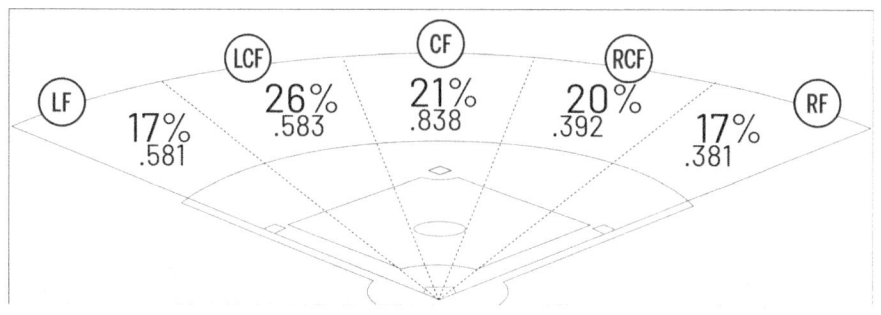

Strike Zone vs LHP

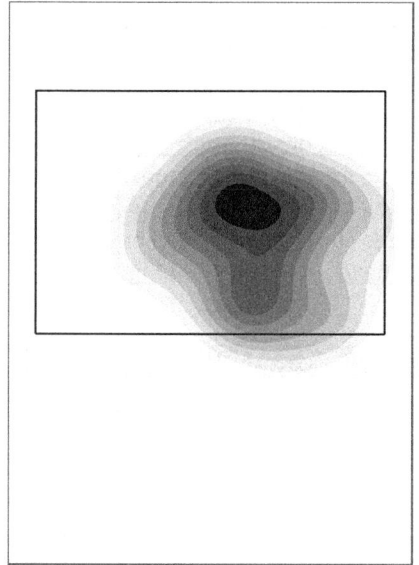

Strike Zone vs RHP

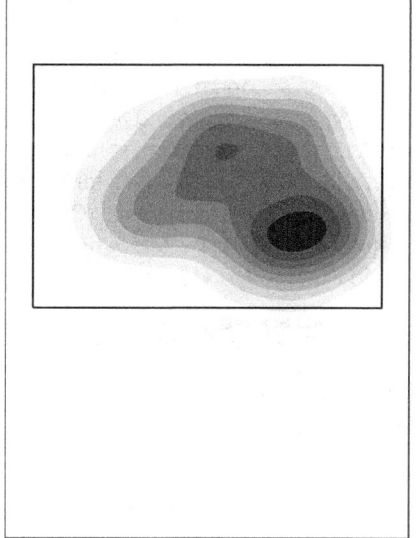

Arizona Diamondbacks 2019

Alex Avila   C

Born: 01/29/87   Age: 32   Bats: L   Throws: R
Height: 5'11"   Weight: 210   Origin: Round 5, 2008 Draft (#163 overall)

YEAR	TEAM	LVL	AGE	PA	R	2B	3B	HR	RBI	BB	K	SB	CS	AVG/OBP/SLG
2016	CHA	MLB	29	209	19	6	0	7	11	38	78	0	0	.213/.359/.373
2017	DET	MLB	30	264	30	11	0	11	32	43	80	0	1	.274/.394/.475
2017	CHN	MLB	30	112	11	2	1	3	17	19	40	0	0	.239/.369/.380
2018	ARI	MLB	31	234	13	6	0	7	20	37	90	0	0	.165/.299/.304
2019	ARI	MLB	32	217	24	7	1	6	22	28	72	0	0	.215/.319/.360

Breakout: 3%   Improve: 27%   Collapse: 25%   Attrition: 26%   MLB: 91%
Comparables: Chris Snyder, Jarrod Saltalamacchia, Jason LaRue

Avila's career trajectory has been consistently up and down. One year he looks like an All-Star, the next a backup. The Diamondbacks received the latter in 2018 and it was so bad at times that fans were actively booing him in his own park. He managed just 17 hits in the first half while playing 50

YEAR	TEAM	P. COUNT	FRM RUNS	BLK RUNS	THRW RUNS	TOT RUNS
2016	CHA	7394	-4.2	0.0	-0.6	-4.7
2017	DET	6716	-5.8	0.7	0.2	-4.8
2017	CHN	3507	-3.3	-0.2	0.0	-3.2
2018	ARI	7984	3.7	0.3	0.0	4.3
2019	ARI	6862	-2.6	0.1	-0.2	-2.6

games. The second half was better, but not exactly good. With Jeff Mathis and John Ryan Murphy around, Avila struggled to get consistent playing time and that's ... well, that's saying something. If there's a glimmer of hope, it might be that Avila has shown a knack for turning things around and never gave up over the course of a painful season. Can he salvage some value in 2019 before his deal runs out? He'd better, or he might just have a hard time finding employment beyond next season.

YEAR	TEAM	LVL	AGE	PA	DRC+	VORP	BABIP	BRR	FRAA	WARP
2016	CHA	MLB	29	209	87	8.3	.341	-2.2	C(54): -5.7	-0.1
2017	DET	MLB	30	264	107	16.2	.380	-1.5	C(50): -0.5, 1B(16): -0.9	1.0
2017	CHN	MLB	30	112	107	5.6	.388	0.5	C(28): 0.2, 1B(3): 0.2	0.7
2018	ARI	MLB	31	234	62	-0.2	.253	-1.4	C(61): 3.2, 1B(3): 0.0	0.2
2019	ARI	MLB	32	217	90	6.3	.308	-0.4	C -4	0.2

Alex Avila, continued

Batted Ball Distribution

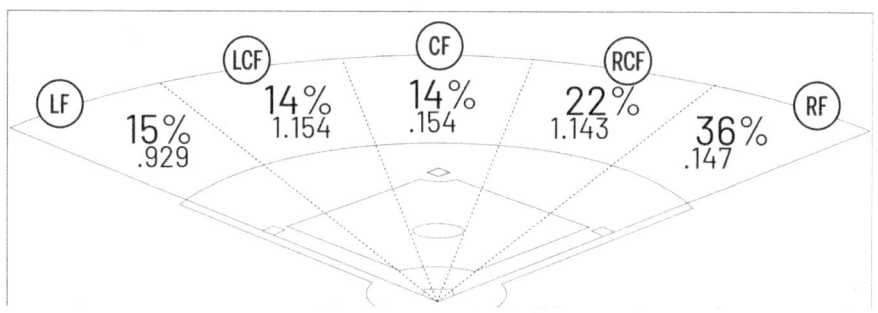

Strike Zone vs LHP

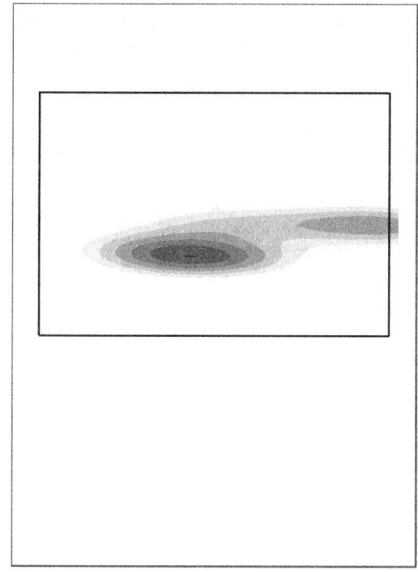

Strike Zone vs RHP

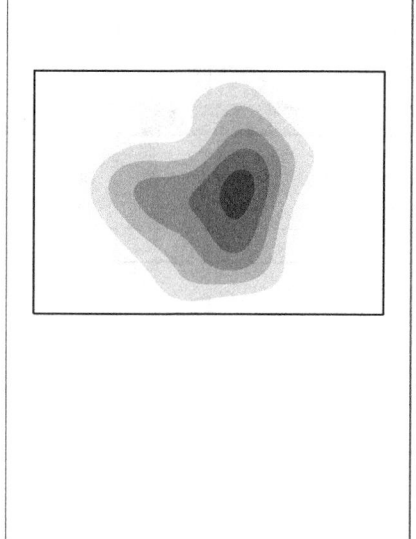

Arizona Diamondbacks 2019

Jarrod Dyson CF

Born: 08/15/84   Age: 34   Bats: L   Throws: R
Height: 5'10"   Weight: 165   Origin: Round 50, 2006 Draft (#1475 overall)

YEAR	TEAM	LVL	AGE	PA	R	2B	3B	HR	RBI	BB	K	SB	CS	AVG/OBP/SLG
2016	KCA	MLB	31	337	46	14	8	1	25	26	39	30	7	.278/.340/.388
2017	SEA	MLB	32	390	56	13	3	5	30	28	55	28	7	.251/.324/.350
2018	ARI	MLB	33	237	29	4	2	2	12	27	34	16	3	.189/.282/.257
2019	ARI	MLB	34	62	8	2	1	1	5	5	10	5	1	.255/.328/.382

Breakout: 0%   Improve: 27%   Collapse: 13%   Attrition: 19%   MLB: 83%
Comparables: Dave Roberts, Sam Fuld, Jacoby Ellsbury

Dyson has never made his living as a hitter. That's just not his game, as his Twitter handle (@mrzoombiya) indicates. A move to the desert could have, in theory, given him a boost. Instead, he dried up even by his own standards. A jump in hard-hit balls weirdly didn't do his BABIP any favors before his season prematurely ended in early July. He'll enter 2019 as a 34-year-old bench outfielder recovering from a down season and groin surgery. Still, he has a year left on his deal and the Diamondbacks' cache of outfielders, particularly those capable of covering center field, instills little confidence. He'll get another shot to extend his playing days and hope for better results, even if just by a little.

YEAR	TEAM	LVL	AGE	PA	DRC+	VORP	BABIP	BRR	FRAA	WARP
2016	KCA	MLB	31	337	86	7.1	.315	1.7	CF(57): 0.4, RF(21): 3.7	1.1
2017	SEA	MLB	32	390	80	3.0	.285	0.0	CF(96): 5.6, LF(12): 3.2	1.2
2018	ARI	MLB	33	237	70	-3.7	.216	2.6	CF(41): 3.3, RF(18): 0.0	0.6
2019	ARI	MLB	34	62	78	0.7	.283	0.7	CF 0, RF 0	0.1

Jarrod Dyson, continued

Batted Ball Distribution

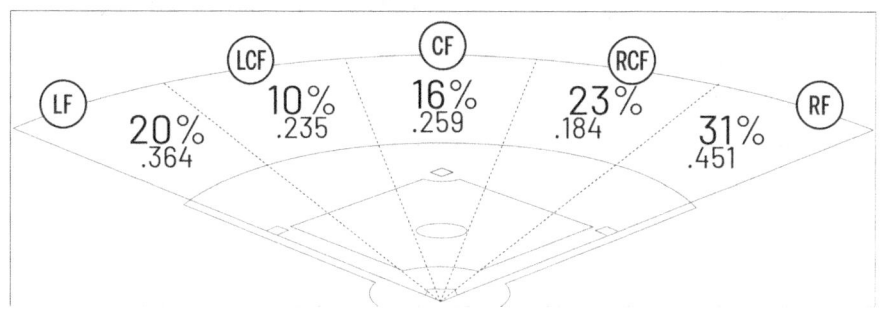

Strike Zone vs LHP

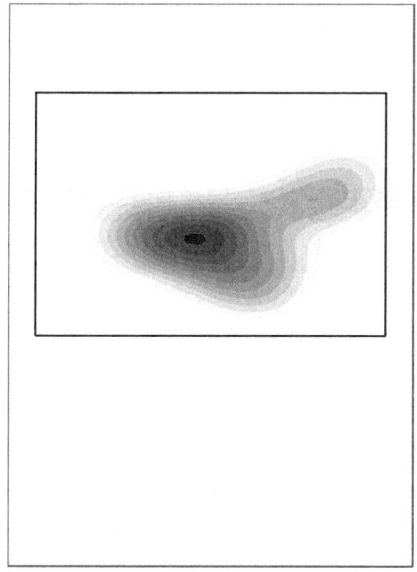

Strike Zone vs RHP

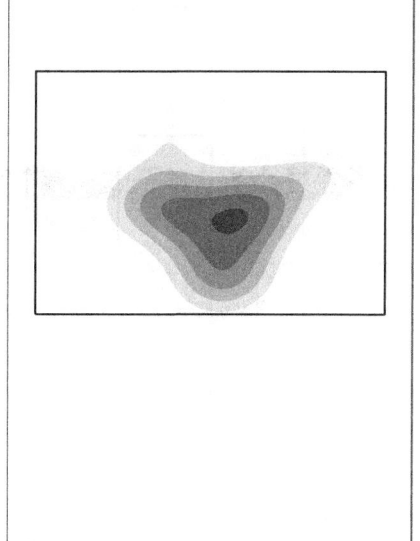

Eduardo Escobar 3B

Born: 01/05/89   Age: 30   Bats: B   Throws: R
Height: 5'10"   Weight: 185   Origin: International Free Agent, 2006

YEAR	TEAM	LVL	AGE	PA	R	2B	3B	HR	RBI	BB	K	SB	CS	AVG/OBP/SLG
2016	MIN	MLB	27	377	32	14	2	6	37	21	72	1	3	.236/.280/.338
2017	MIN	MLB	28	499	62	16	5	21	73	33	98	5	1	.254/.309/.449
2018	MIN	MLB	29	408	45	37	3	15	63	34	91	1	3	.274/.338/.514
2018	ARI	MLB	29	223	30	11	0	8	21	18	35	1	1	.268/.327/.444
2019	ARI	MLB	30	561	62	29	3	17	68	43	110	4	3	.259/.322/.429

Breakout: 2%   Improve: 40%   Collapse: 15%   Attrition: 7%   MLB: 95%
Comparables: Joe Crede, Scott Brosius, Billy Johnson

Two seasons ago, the Diamondbacks cashed in at the deadline on #JustDingers in J.D. Martinez. Last season, they cashed in at the deadline on #JustDoubles in Escobar. While the hashtag didn't take off, Escobar did during his time in Sedona Red. He filled in well for an injured Jake Lamb down the stretch and established his late-blooming excellence. He's roughly average at third base, but he hits well enough to justify everyday reps somewhere in the infield. After inking a three-year extension, he'll do just that for the Diamondbacks — a team that is always in need of inexpensive production. They'll hope his productive audition wasn't a fluke and that those doubles just keep coming, even if that requires moving him around defensively.

YEAR	TEAM	LVL	AGE	PA	DRC+	VORP	BABIP	BRR	FRAA	WARP
2016	MIN	MLB	27	377	75	-3.3	.280	1.7	SS(71): 1.0, 3B(23): -1.2	0.5
2017	MIN	MLB	28	499	100	14.8	.279	2.3	3B(79): -5.1, SS(16): -0.5	1.3
2018	MIN	MLB	29	408	115	26.7	.325	-0.1	3B(77): -2.1, SS(21): 0.0	2.1
2018	ARI	MLB	29	223	114	12.0	.281	0.5	3B(54): -4.9	0.8
2019	ARI	MLB	30	561	101	18.3	.297	-1.0	3B -6, SS -1	0.8

Eduardo Escobar, continued

Batted Ball Distribution

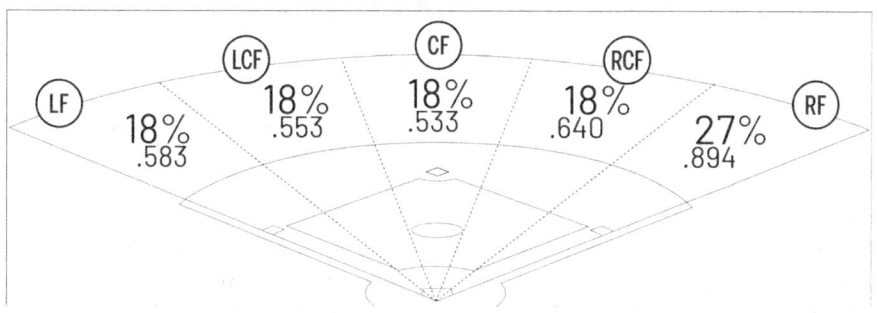

Strike Zone vs LHP

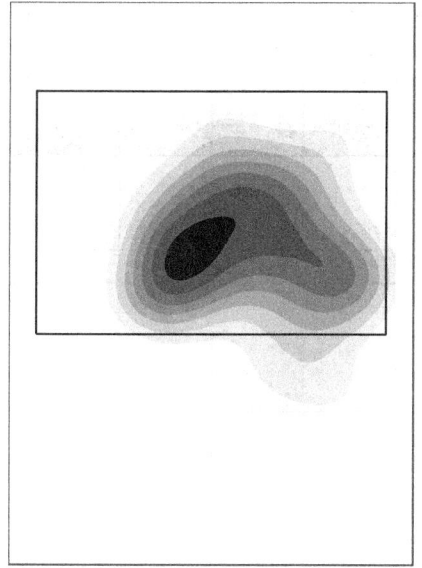

Strike Zone vs RHP

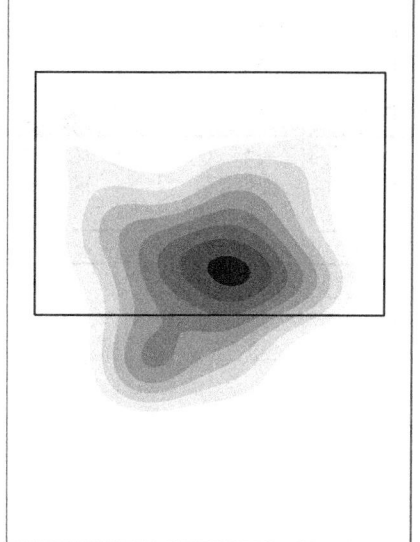

Arizona Diamondbacks 2019

Wilmer Flores INF
Born: 08/06/91   Age: 27   Bats: R   Throws: R
Height: 6'3"   Weight: 205   Origin: International Free Agent, 2007

YEAR	TEAM	LVL	AGE	PA	R	2B	3B	HR	RBI	BB	K	SB	CS	AVG/OBP/SLG
2016	NYN	MLB	24	335	38	14	0	16	49	23	48	1	1	.267/.319/.469
2017	NYN	MLB	25	362	42	17	1	18	52	17	54	1	1	.271/.307/.488
2018	NYN	MLB	26	429	43	25	0	11	51	29	42	0	0	.267/.319/.417
2019	ARI	MLB	27	473	54	25	2	16	61	35	65	1	1	.273/.332/.452

Breakout: 4%   Improve: 47%   Collapse: 13%   Attrition: 8%   MLB: 97%
Comparables: James Loney, Eddie Waitkus, Eric Hosmer

This man is trying to break your heart. Despite playing for a team owned by, to put it bluntly, grifters and meddlers, Flores loves the New York Metropolitans in a way that puts most fans of the team to shame. He put up his typical season despite playing through various injuries. He continued to be jerked around in terms of playing time despite being the team's best right-handed hitting option at two or three positions. The Mets remained noncommittal about his future in blue and orange with free agency looming—all the way up until he received the diagnosis that he has early-onset arthritis in both of his knees, which ended his season early, and was likely why he was non-tendered. He does not deserve this.

YEAR	TEAM	LVL	AGE	PA	DRC+	VORP	BABIP	BRR	FRAA	WARP
2016	NYN	MLB	24	335	117	21.9	.268	-2.4	3B(51): -4.0, 1B(27): 0.4	1.2
2017	NYN	MLB	25	362	112	15.8	.270	-0.6	3B(55): 0.2, 1B(29): -0.2	1.5
2018	NYN	MLB	26	429	106	13.0	.269	-3.2	1B(83): -2.6, 2B(13): 0.1	0.4
2019	ARI	MLB	27	473	109	20.4	.287	-0.8	2B 0	2.1

Wilmer Flores, continued

Batted Ball Distribution

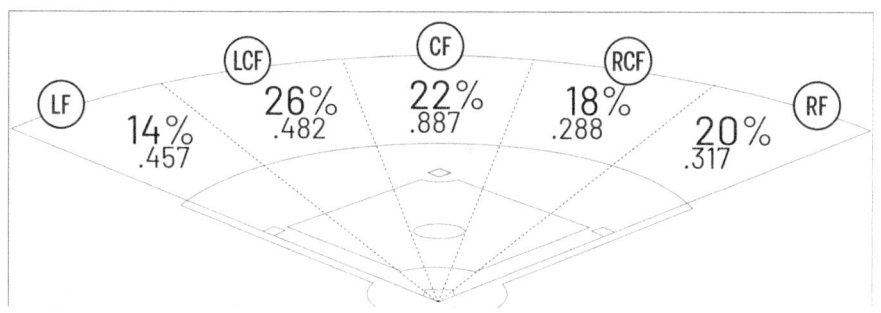

Strike Zone vs LHP

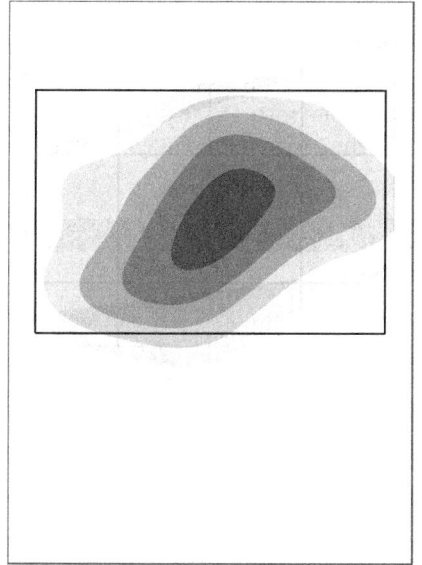

Strike Zone vs RHP

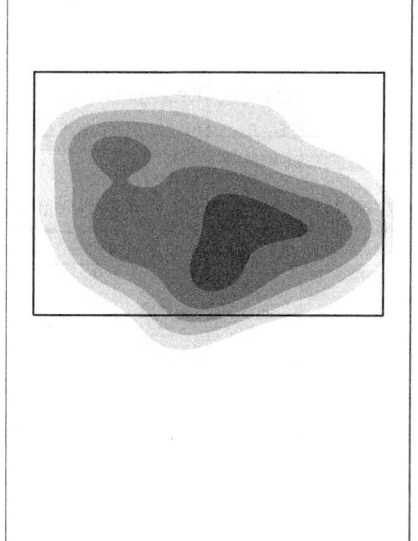

Arizona Diamondbacks 2019

Adam Jones CF
Born: 08/01/85 Age: 33 Bats: R Throws: R
Height: 6'2" Weight: 215 Origin: Round 1, 2003 Draft (#37 overall)

YEAR	TEAM	LVL	AGE	PA	R	2B	3B	HR	RBI	BB	K	SB	CS	AVG/OBP/SLG
2016	BAL	MLB	30	672	86	19	0	29	83	39	115	2	0	.265/.310/.436
2017	BAL	MLB	31	635	82	28	1	26	73	27	113	2	1	.285/.322/.466
2018	BAL	MLB	32	613	54	35	0	15	63	24	93	7	1	.281/.313/.419
2019	ARI	MLB	33	279	34	13	1	8	30	17	48	2	0	.268/.319/.420

Breakout: 0% Improve: 29% Collapse: 26% Attrition: 13% MLB: 99%
Comparables: Bing Miller, Willie Davis, Al Oliver

There is only so much control a baseball player has. He can't control where he's drafted, or where he goes for first few years of his career. He can't control how much ownership spends, who his teammates are, or the conditions in which he plays. Only a select few can control whether or not they're traded. Adam Jones elected to exercise what control he has this year when he refused a deadline trade, opting instead to finish out his ten-year Orioles career on his terms. The 33-year-old will be able to control where he signs as a free agent this winter. While his days as a center fielder seem past him, Jones can still play a respectable corner outfield, and although his power numbers took an enormous dip in 2018, the decline was so steep as to suggest a resurgence is possible for a team willing to gamble that Jones is closer to the 25-home run player he's been over the past half-decade plus.

YEAR	TEAM	LVL	AGE	PA	DRC+	VORP	BABIP	BRR	FRAA	WARP
2016	BAL	MLB	30	672	107	17.4	.280	2.7	CF(152): 4.4	3.6
2017	BAL	MLB	31	635	106	28.1	.312	3.4	CF(147): -4.7	2.6
2018	BAL	MLB	32	613	99	12.8	.311	1.0	CF(106): -11.8, RF(33): 2.0	1.0
2019	ARI	MLB	33	279	96	9.3	.301	-0.2	CF -1, LF 0	0.6

Adam Jones, continued

Batted Ball Distribution

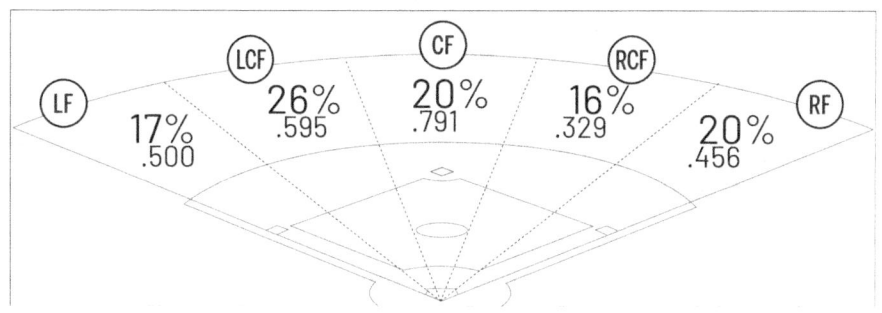

Strike Zone vs LHP

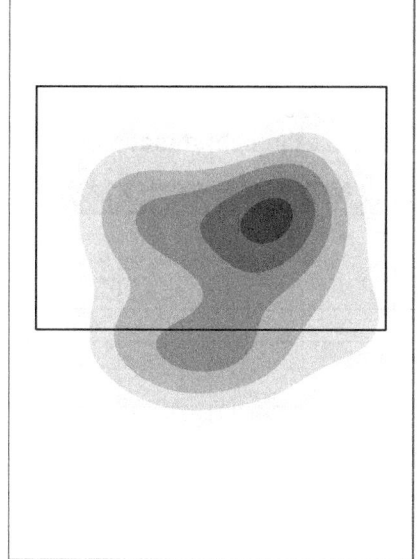

Strike Zone vs RHP

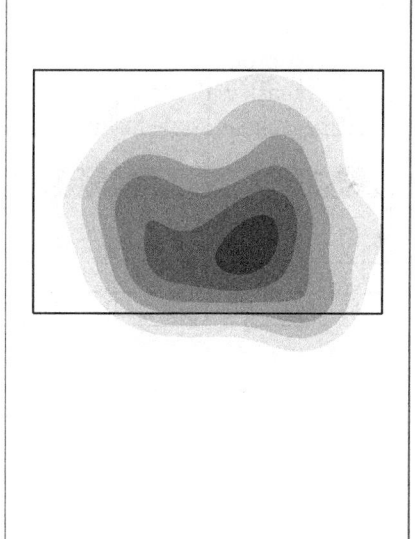

Jake Lamb 3B

Born: 10/09/90 Age: 28 Bats: L Throws: R
Height: 6'3" Weight: 215 Origin: Round 6, 2012 Draft (#213 overall)

YEAR	TEAM	LVL	AGE	PA	R	2B	3B	HR	RBI	BB	K	SB	CS	AVG/OBP/SLG
2016	ARI	MLB	25	594	81	31	9	29	91	64	154	6	1	.249/.332/.509
2017	ARI	MLB	26	635	89	30	4	30	105	87	152	6	4	.248/.357/.487
2018	ARI	MLB	27	238	34	8	0	6	31	26	65	1	2	.222/.307/.348
2019	ARI	MLB	28	612	83	27	4	23	71	69	152	5	3	.240/.331/.434

Breakout: 11% Improve: 59% Collapse: 12% Attrition: 8% MLB: 96%
Comparables: Todd Frazier, Travis Shaw, Chase Headley

Lamb is no longer a mystery. At his best, he's a low-to-medium-average hitter capable of sending pitches from righties into orbit and eking out a hit or two versus lefties. At his worst, he's not much more than a replacement-level player. He's run hot and cold for a few seasons now, often scorching the first half and going ice cold in the second. He didn't have a chance to tank in the second half of 2018, however, because a) he had already tanked to start the year and, b) got hurt just after the All-Star break, not to return. Shoulder injuries are weird and it's unclear how Lamb recovers. The Diamondbacks hedged their bets by signing the versatile, productive Eduardo Escobar to an extension. Lamb presumably has a short leash with the organization. He may end up being platooned (finally), or let go in some fashion as his salary rises through arbitration.

YEAR	TEAM	LVL	AGE	PA	DRC+	VORP	BABIP	BRR	FRAA	WARP
2016	ARI	MLB	25	594	105	37.8	.294	2.3	3B(142): -5.0	2.2
2017	ARI	MLB	26	635	119	44.8	.287	2.0	3B(144): -10.8	2.9
2018	ARI	MLB	27	238	80	10.3	.286	1.6	3B(52): -3.7	0.0
2019	ARI	MLB	28	612	109	21.7	.289	-0.6	1B -1, 3B -2	1.6

Jake Lamb, continued

Batted Ball Distribution

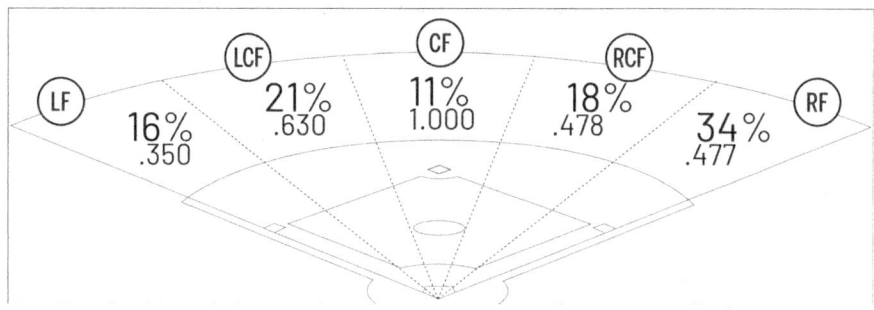

Strike Zone vs LHP   **Strike Zone vs RHP**

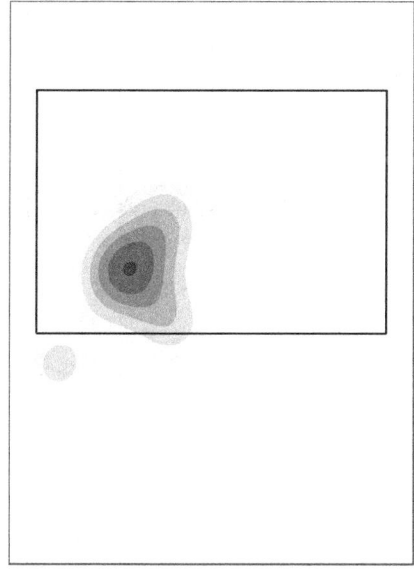
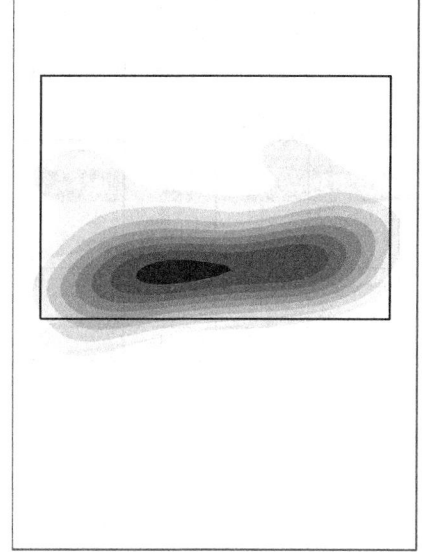

Arizona Diamondbacks 2019

Ketel Marte 2B
Born: 10/12/93   Age: 25   Bats: B   Throws: R
Height: 6'1"   Weight: 165   Origin: International Free Agent, 2010

YEAR	TEAM	LVL	AGE	PA	R	2B	3B	HR	RBI	BB	K	SB	CS	AVG/OBP/SLG
2016	SEA	MLB	22	466	55	21	2	1	33	18	84	11	5	.259/.287/.323
2017	RNO	AAA	23	338	62	23	7	6	41	25	34	7	2	.338/.391/.514
2017	ARI	MLB	23	255	30	11	2	5	18	29	37	3	1	.260/.345/.395
2018	ARI	MLB	24	580	68	26	12	14	59	54	79	6	1	.260/.332/.437
2019	ARI	MLB	25	516	56	24	6	11	57	41	79	8	3	.266/.329/.414

Breakout: 4%   Improve: 61%   Collapse: 7%   Attrition: 11%   MLB: 98%
Comparables: Kolten Wong, Blake DeWitt, Aaron Hill

It's easy to forget that Marte is still really young. With four seasons under his belt, he's coming off an age-24 season in which he put up his best numbers to date. He set career-highs in nearly every meaningful offensive category while also signing an extension that will guarantee that he remains affordable for years to come. His defensive versatility is a nice bonus, but perhaps more than anything, it's the way Marte plays that's most exciting. He's a tough dude who seems to think he's about six inches taller than he really is, battles every day and gives the kind of effort that has quickly made him a favorite among Diamondbacks fans. There's still room for improvement, and given his age, the #MartePartay might just be getting started.

YEAR	TEAM	LVL	AGE	PA	DRC+	VORP	BABIP	BRR	FRAA	WARP
2016	SEA	MLB	22	466	66	2.5	.313	2.6	SS(119): -1.5	0.2
2017	RNO	AAA	23	338	127	31.4	.365	3.8	SS(59): 2.1, CF(5): 1.6	2.9
2017	ARI	MLB	23	255	100	14.0	.290	1.5	SS(64): -0.1, 3B(3): 0.1	1.3
2018	ARI	MLB	24	580	102	27.4	.282	0.6	2B(131): 4.5, SS(28): 1.8	2.9
2019	ARI	MLB	25	516	100	22.0	.295	0.7	CF 0, SS 0	2.0

Ketel Marte, continued

Batted Ball Distribution

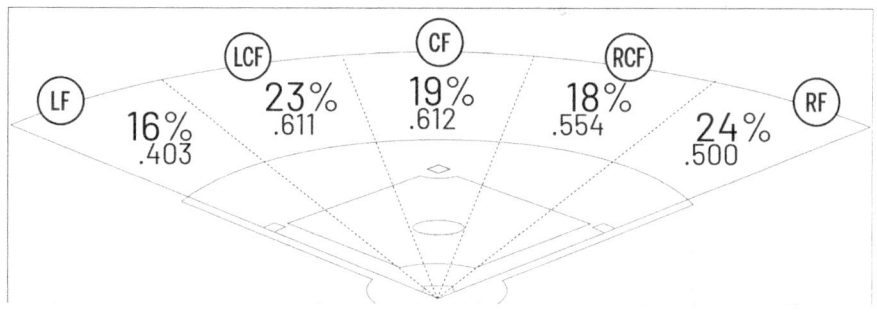

Strike Zone vs LHP

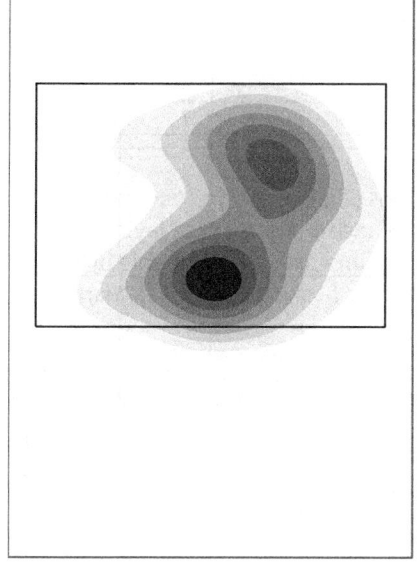

Strike Zone vs RHP

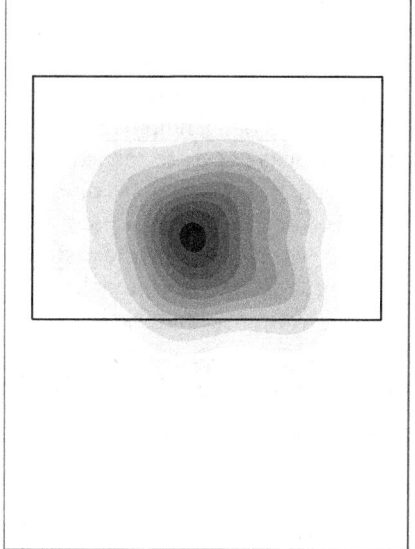

John Ryan Murphy C

Born: 05/13/91   Age: 28   Bats: R   Throws: R
Height: 5'11"   Weight: 205   Origin: Round 2, 2009 Draft (#76 overall)

YEAR	TEAM	LVL	AGE	PA	R	2B	3B	HR	RBI	BB	K	SB	CS	AVG/OBP/SLG
2016	ROC	AAA	25	290	24	14	0	3	39	21	51	0	0	.236/.286/.323
2016	MIN	MLB	25	90	4	3	0	1	3	5	19	0	0	.146/.193/.220
2017	ROC	AAA	26	218	21	9	0	4	27	22	36	0	0	.222/.298/.330
2017	RNO	AAA	26	75	5	0	0	2	7	7	7	0	0	.284/.351/.373
2017	ARI	MLB	26	7	0	1	0	0	1	0	1	0	0	.143/.143/.286
2018	ARI	MLB	27	223	19	9	0	9	24	11	71	0	0	.202/.244/.375
2019	ARI	MLB	28	143	14	5	1	4	15	10	33	0	0	.215/.275/.362

Breakout: 9%   Improve: 40%   Collapse: 12%   Attrition: 42%   MLB: 78%
Comparables: Mike Rabelo, Jason Jaramillo, Austin Romine

Never trust a man with two first names. It's not clear if you can trust a man with *three* first names, but if Murphy provides any clues the answer is still probably no. He was an under-the-radar pickup by Mike Hazen toward the tail end of 2017 and started 2018 off with a bang, helping the Diamondbacks decide to carry three catchers all year. Seven of his nine home runs came in the first two months of the season and he eventually lost any semblance of significant playing time to the other two catchers on the roster. Murphy appeared to be capable of providing some offensive punch, but instead he broke the D-backs' heart and they may never trust him again.

YEAR	TEAM	P. COUNT	FRM RUNS	BLK RUNS	THRW RUNS	TOT RUNS
2016	MIN	3340	1.4	-1.7	0.1	-0.2
2017	ARI	249	0.1	0.1	0.0	0.2
2017	ROC	6992	21.3	-0.2	0.6	21.3
2017	RNO	2920	0.0	-0.6	0.7	-0.1
2018	ARI	7566	9.3	0.3	-0.1	9.9
2019	ARI	4849	5.7	-0.5	0.0	5.3

YEAR	TEAM	LVL	AGE	PA	DRC+	VORP	BABIP	BRR	FRAA	WARP
2016	ROC	AAA	25	290	77	2.0	.274	-1.4	C(80): 17.8	1.9
2016	MIN	MLB	25	90	67	-5.2	.175	-0.3	C(25): -0.6	0.0
2017	ROC	AAA	26	218	84	2.5	.250	1.0	C(53): 1.2	0.5
2017	RNO	AAA	26	75	96	2.2	.293	-0.4	C(19): -0.2	0.2
2017	ARI	MLB	26	7	79	-1.3	.167	-0.1	C(5): 0.2	0.0
2018	ARI	MLB	27	223	70	1.6	.256	-1.0	C(68): 10.2	1.2
2019	ARI	MLB	28	143	60	-0.6	.254	-0.2	C 5	0.4

John Ryan Murphy, continued

Batted Ball Distribution

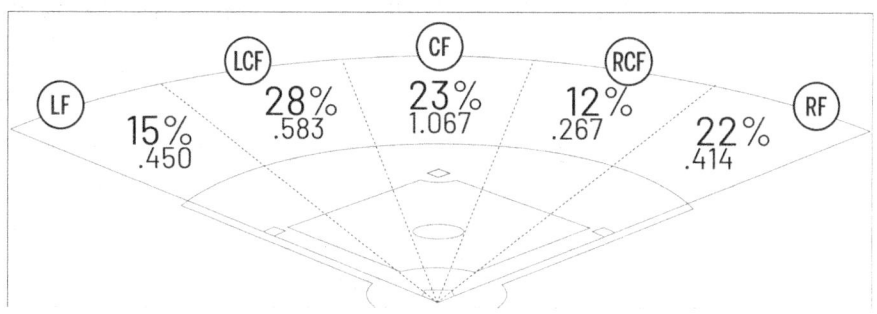

Strike Zone vs LHP   Strike Zone vs RHP

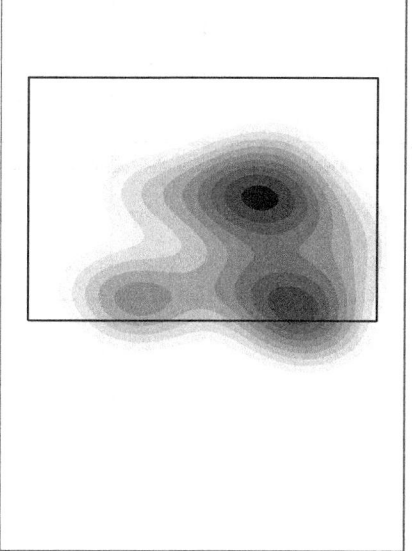

Arizona Diamondbacks 2019

David Peralta LF
Born: 08/14/87   Age: 31   Bats: L   Throws: L
Height: 6'1"   Weight: 210   Origin: International Free Agent, 2005

YEAR	TEAM	LVL	AGE	PA	R	2B	3B	HR	RBI	BB	K	SB	CS	AVG/OBP/SLG
2016	ARI	MLB	28	183	23	9	5	4	15	8	42	2	0	.251/.295/.433
2017	ARI	MLB	29	577	82	31	3	14	57	43	94	8	4	.293/.352/.444
2018	ARI	MLB	30	614	75	25	5	30	87	48	124	4	0	.293/.352/.516
2019	ARI	MLB	31	586	75	26	4	18	64	44	117	6	2	.265/.326/.430

Breakout: 0%   Improve: 36%   Collapse: 11%   Attrition: 9%   MLB: 90%
Comparables: Juan Rivera, Carl Crawford, David Murphy

A winding career path for Peralta has brought plenty of surprises, not all of them good, but damn if he wasn't low-key excellent again in 2018. He often flies under the radar, but Peralta hit the 30-home run mark for the first time as neither opposing pitchers nor the humidor could hold him down. The defense isn't great, but it's fine for left field and he still has that cannon of an arm that once made him a prized pitching prospect. Peralta is a sneaky good player who has provided value beyond his compensation on multiple occasions—exactly what the Diamondbacks covet. He's on the wrong side of 30, however, and despite a delayed start to his big-league career, the real focus will be on how long he can keep it going. For now, the Freight Train appears to have plenty of momentum.

YEAR	TEAM	LVL	AGE	PA	DRC+	VORP	BABIP	BRR	FRAA	WARP
2016	ARI	MLB	28	183	77	4.7	.310	2.4	RF(44): 0.0, CF(8): -0.4	0.1
2017	ARI	MLB	29	577	103	24.6	.333	-0.9	RF(78): 10.0, LF(50): 2.2	2.7
2018	ARI	MLB	30	614	121	40.0	.328	1.2	LF(138): -11.0, RF(5): -0.5	2.1
2019	ARI	MLB	31	586	102	20.0	.305	-0.1	LF -4	1.4

David Peralta, continued

Batted Ball Distribution

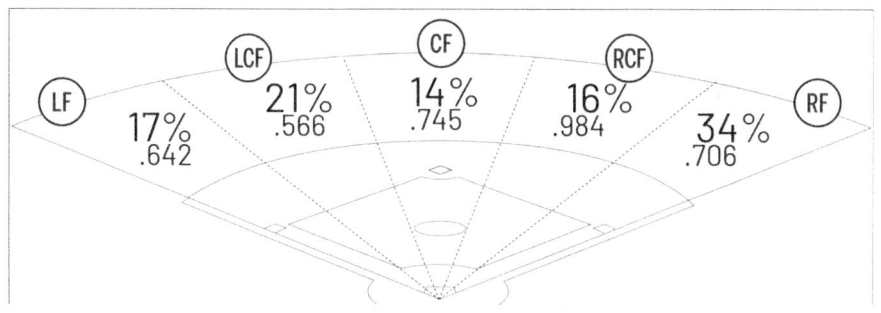

Strike Zone vs LHP   **Strike Zone vs RHP**

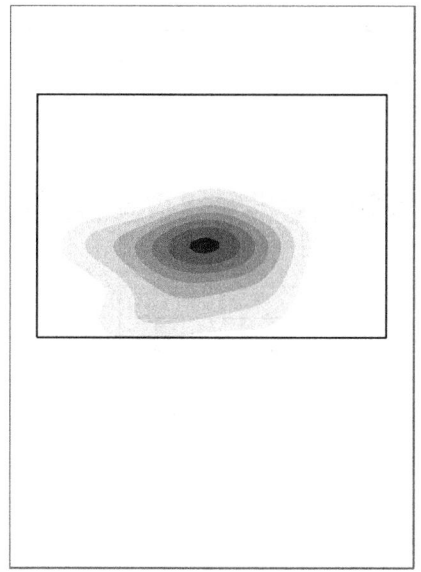 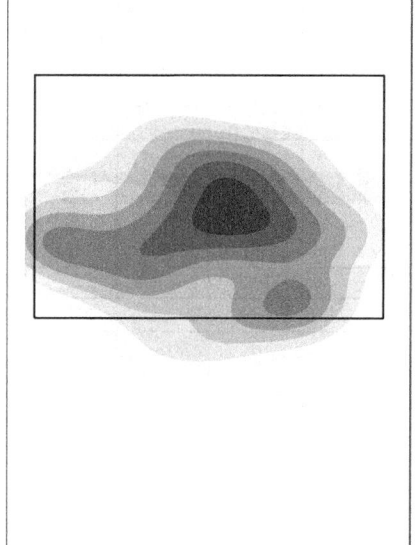

Arizona Diamondbacks 2019

Steven Souza RF

Born: 04/24/89 Age: 30 Bats: R Throws: R
Height: 6'4" Weight: 225 Origin: Round 3, 2007 Draft (#100 overall)

YEAR	TEAM	LVL	AGE	PA	R	2B	3B	HR	RBI	BB	K	SB	CS	AVG/OBP/SLG
2016	TBA	MLB	27	468	58	17	1	17	49	31	159	7	6	.247/.303/.409
2017	TBA	MLB	28	617	78	21	2	30	78	84	179	16	4	.239/.351/.459
2018	ARI	MLB	29	272	21	15	3	5	29	28	75	6	1	.220/.309/.369
2019	ARI	MLB	30	475	59	19	3	16	57	51	135	11	4	.240/.329/.416

Breakout: 2% Improve: 48% Collapse: 17% Attrition: 13% MLB: 100%
Comparables: Jayson Werth, Brad Hawpe, Will Venable

In Charles Dickens' masterpiece *Great Expectations*, Pip rises to great wealth and leaves his old life behind before watching it all come crashing down due to his own arrogance. There's a metaphor in there somewhere in regard to the Diamondbacks' treatment of the outfield. They waved goodbye to J.D. Martinez and thought they had an adequate replacement in Souza before his season got downright weird. He hit to the opposite field more in 2018 and his fly balls lost a lot of their effectiveness, as his swing and approach produced new and damning results. All is not lost, however. Souza tried to revert back to form late in the season and the results picked up some. With two years of team control remaining, the Diamondbacks will hope to salvage something from their oft-criticized decision.

YEAR	TEAM	LVL	AGE	PA	DRC+	VORP	BABIP	BRR	FRAA	WARP
2016	TBA	MLB	27	468	87	6.8	.348	2.3	RF(111): -1.9, CF(3): 0.2	0.3
2017	TBA	MLB	28	617	116	27.3	.302	-1.9	RF(138): -6.8, CF(3): -0.5	1.6
2018	ARI	MLB	29	272	77	-0.5	.298	0.1	RF(65): -5.9, CF(1): 0.0	-0.8
2019	ARI	MLB	30	475	100	13.8	.312	0.7	RF -5	0.7

Steven Souza, continued

Batted Ball Distribution

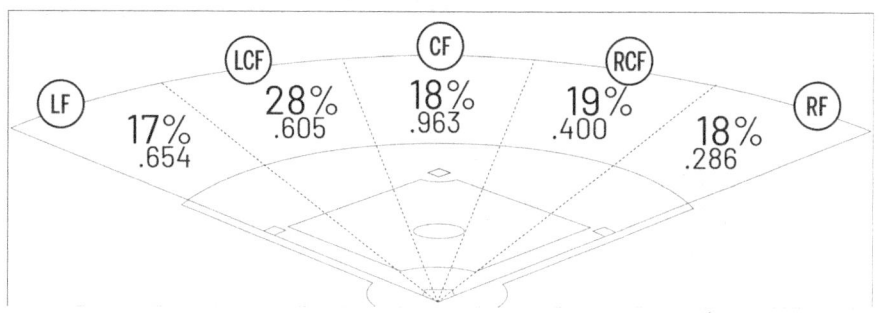

Strike Zone vs LHP

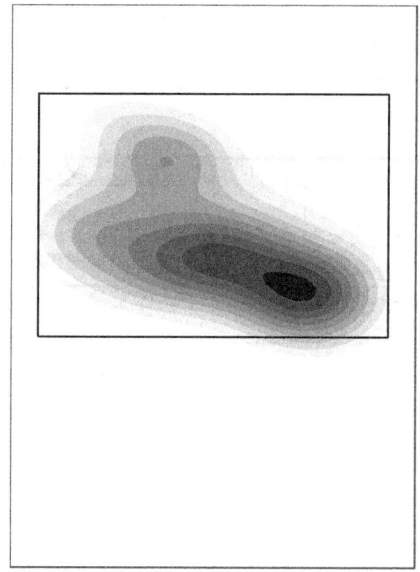

Strike Zone vs RHP

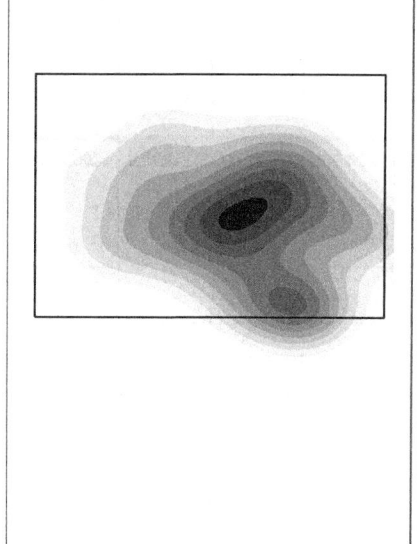

Arizona Diamondbacks 2019

Matt Andriese RHP

Born: 08/28/89 Age: 29 Bats: R Throws: R
Height: 6'2" Weight: 225 Origin: Round 3, 2011 Draft (#112 overall)

YEAR	TEAM	LVL	AGE	W	L	SV	G	GS	IP	H	HR	BB/9	K/9	K	GB%	BABIP
2016	DUR	AAA	26	1	2	0	6	6	34¹	32	2	1.8	11.5	44	48%	.345
2016	TBA	MLB	26	8	8	1	29	19	127²	131	17	1.8	7.7	109	44%	.305
2017	TBA	MLB	27	5	5	1	18	17	86	90	16	2.9	8.0	76	46%	.296
2018	TBA	MLB	28	3	4	0	27	4	59²	55	7	2.7	8.9	59	52%	.291
2018	ARI	MLB	28	0	3	0	14	1	19	29	8	3.3	9.0	19	44%	.382
2019	ARI	MLB	29	3	3	0	45	5	62	58	6	3.1	9.0	63	46%	.298

Breakout: 32% Improve: 52% Collapse: 19% Attrition: 25% MLB: 83%
Comparables: Matt Belisle, Chase Anderson, Vidal Nuno

When the Diamondbacks tried to address their needs at the 2018 trade deadline, they acquired Andriese from the Rays. He wasn't a clear upgrade and was coming from a non-traditional pitching scheme, but he made sense in a strange way. Other players on the roster were approaching free agency with demands that the Diamondbacks likely couldn't bargain for and Andriese was a long play to fill out the rotation in future. And while he didn't do much to help the team's postseason chances in the immediate, he should provide affordable depth moving forward.

YEAR	TEAM	LVL	AGE	WHIP	ERA	DRA	WARP	MPH	FB%	WHF	CSP
2016	DUR	AAA	26	1.14	3.41	2.37	1.2				
2016	TBA	MLB	26	1.22	4.37	3.63	2.4	93.8	46	11.3	47.2
2017	TBA	MLB	27	1.37	4.50	4.10	1.4	93.5	44.3	11.8	48.2
2018	TBA	MLB	28	1.22	4.07	4.89	0.1	93.8	48.9	12.8	48.5
2018	ARI	MLB	28	1.89	9.00	5.20	0.0	93.7	48.9	14.3	48
2019	ARI	MLB	29	1.27	3.60	4.03	0.6	93.0	46.5	12.1	48

Matt Andriese, continued

Pitch Shape vs LHH

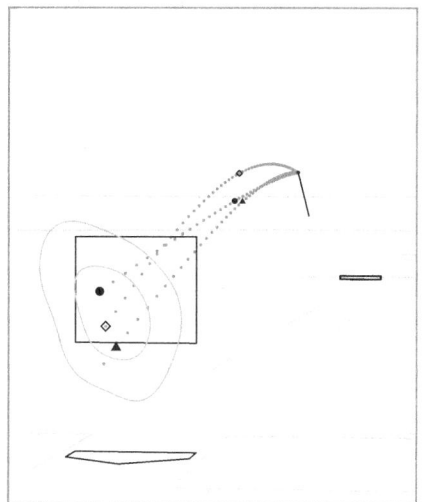

Pitch Shape vs RHH

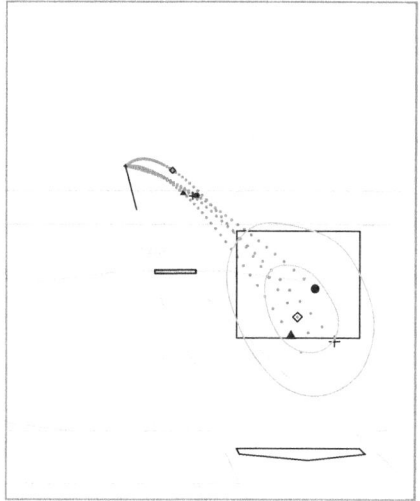

Type	Frequency	Velocity	H Movement	V Movement
● Fastball	46.8%	92.8 [101]	-5.9 [104]	-13.5 [107]
☐ Sinker				
+ Cutter	4.4%	86.9 [89]	0.4 [91]	-30.4 [73]
▲ Changeup	40.1%	86.7 [105]	-4.3 [137]	-31.9 [86]
✕ Splitter				
▽ Slider				
◇ Curveball	8.7%	81.3 [110]	5.2 [89]	-48 [100]
⊕ Slow Curveball				
✻ Knuckleball				
▼ Screwball				

Arizona Diamondbacks 2019

Silvino Bracho RHP
Born: 07/17/92   Age: 26   Bats: R   Throws: R
Height: 5'10"   Weight: 190   Origin: International Free Agent, 2011

YEAR	TEAM	LVL	AGE	W	L	SV	G	GS	IP	H	HR	BB/9	K/9	K	GB%	BABIP
2016	RNO	AAA	23	0	2	15	36	0	33²	34	2	2.1	11.5	43	28%	.352
2016	ARI	MLB	23	0	2	0	26	0	24²	31	7	3.6	6.2	17	29%	.293
2017	RNO	AAA	24	3	2	8	33	0	35¹	25	8	4.3	12.2	48	34%	.239
2017	ARI	MLB	24	0	0	0	21	0	20²	18	5	3.0	10.9	25	46%	.260
2018	RNO	AAA	25	2	2	8	27	0	34¹	39	3	2.1	13.6	52	39%	.450
2018	ARI	MLB	25	2	0	0	31	0	31	25	2	3.5	9.9	34	38%	.295
2019	ARI	MLB	26	2	2	0	30	0	32	28	4	3.8	10.6	38	37%	.297

Breakout: 16%   Improve: 34%   Collapse: 20%   Attrition: 24%   MLB: 70%
Comparables: Chasen Shreve, Louis Coleman, Shawn Kelley

Do baseball players get to keep their own airline miles? Sure, most don't need the freebies given their paychecks, but Bracho may disagree. Over the past four seasons, he's been called up 22 times, usually making what must now be a familiar flight from Reno to wherever. Bracho has also yielded balls in play that might qualify for their own frequent flyer miles given his fly-ball tendencies. But after giving up nearly one home run for every four appearances through 2017, he was much more successful at keeping the ball in the park. He might just be in line for a future in the D-backs' bullpen this season, as he's finally out of options.

YEAR	TEAM	LVL	AGE	WHIP	ERA	DRA	WARP	MPH	FB%	WHF	CSP
2016	RNO	AAA	23	1.25	4.81	3.14	0.7				
2016	ARI	MLB	23	1.66	7.30	7.46	-0.7	95.0	64.9	11.6	50.3
2017	RNO	AAA	24	1.19	4.08	3.57	0.7				
2017	ARI	MLB	24	1.21	5.66	3.82	0.3	94.5	50.7	14.3	52
2018	RNO	AAA	25	1.37	4.46	2.10	1.2				
2018	ARI	MLB	25	1.19	3.19	4.12	0.3	94.5	55.6	16.5	49.1
2019	ARI	MLB	26	1.30	4.07	4.41	0.1	94.2	57.7	14.9	51.3

Silvino Bracho, continued

Pitch Shape vs LHH

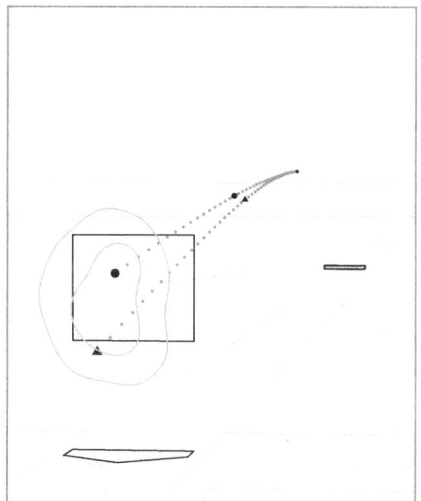

Pitch Shape vs RHH

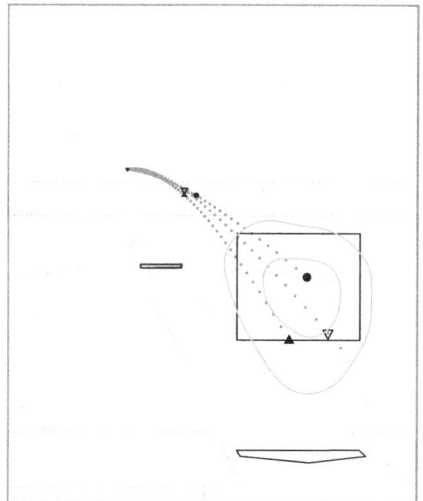

Type	Frequency	Velocity	H Movement	V Movement
● Fastball	55.6%	93.7 [104]	-3.9 [113]	-14 [106]
☐ Sinker				
+ Cutter				
▲ Changeup	36.9%	84.3 [96]	-9.4 [110]	-29 [95]
× Splitter				
▽ Slider	7.5%	83.4 [95]	6 [105]	-33.5 [98]
◇ Curveball				
⊕ Slow Curveball				
✳ Knuckleball				
▼ Screwball				

Arizona Diamondbacks 2019

Archie Bradley   RHP
Born: 08/10/92   Age: 26   Bats: R   Throws: R
Height: 6'4"   Weight: 225   Origin: Round 1, 2011 Draft (#7 overall)

YEAR	TEAM	LVL	AGE	W	L	SV	G	GS	IP	H	HR	BB/9	K/9	K	GB%	BABIP
2016	RNO	AAA	23	5	1	0	7	7	40^2	26	0	4.0	10.4	47	64%	.289
2016	ARI	MLB	23	8	9	0	26	26	141^2	154	16	4.3	9.1	143	47%	.338
2017	ARI	MLB	24	3	3	1	63	0	73	55	4	2.6	9.7	79	49%	.276
2018	ARI	MLB	25	4	5	3	76	0	71^2	62	9	2.5	9.4	75	50%	.282
2019	ARI	MLB	26	3	2	14	51	0	53	44	4	3.6	9.8	58	48%	.291

Breakout: 23%   Improve: 64%   Collapse: 13%   Attrition: 9%   MLB: 88%
Comparables: Yordano Ventura, Trevor Bauer, Gerrit Cole

The yin and the yang. The sun and the moon. Heads and tails. These things are meant to balance out. If you take Bradley's first and second halves, they balance themselves out, too. That "balance" makes for a reliever who hasn't quite turned the corner yet despite lofty expectations. A brilliant first half abruptly gave way to a miserable second half as Bradley took his untimely lumps down the stretch and let several key leads slip away. His command is still problematic and he used his fastball up plenty with occasionally catastrophic results. Problems with his curveball — a pitch that's been nasty in the past but was shelved at times — didn't help. He may still be the closer of the future, but what that future holds seems a toss-up.

YEAR	TEAM	LVL	AGE	WHIP	ERA	DRA	WARP	MPH	FB%	WHF	CSP
2016	RNO	AAA	23	1.08	1.99	3.92	0.7				
2016	ARI	MLB	23	1.56	5.02	5.68	-0.5	95.1	69.2	9.1	48.3
2017	ARI	MLB	24	1.04	1.73	3.88	1.1	98.0	75.6	10.9	52.7
2018	ARI	MLB	25	1.14	3.64	4.48	0.4	97.3	81.7	10	51.3
2019	ARI	MLB	26	1.21	3.04	3.55	0.8	96.2	76.3	10	51.9

Archie Bradley, continued

Pitch Shape vs LHH

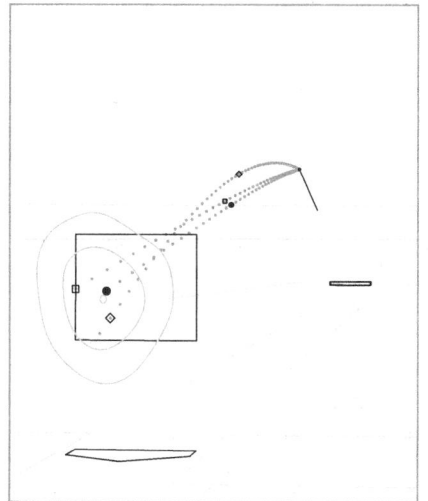

Pitch Shape vs RHH

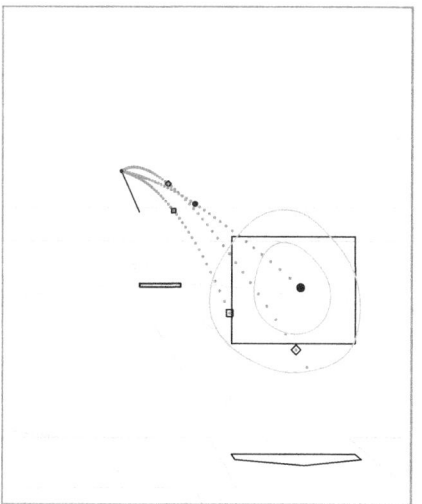

Type	Frequency	Velocity	H Movement	V Movement
● Fastball	69.9%	96.1 [112]	-6.5 [101]	-12.2 [111]
□ Sinker	11.7%	96.1 [118]	-12.5 [101]	-15.2 [117]
+ Cutter	0.6%	88.1 [96]	3.9 [112]	-25.4 [93]
▲ Changeup				
× Splitter				
▽ Slider				
◇ Curveball	17.8%	81.6 [111]	5.1 [89]	-46 [105]
✦ Slow Curveball				
✳ Knuckleball				
▼ Screwball				

Arizona Diamondbacks 2019

Andrew Chafin LHP

Born: 06/17/90 Age: 29 Bats: R Throws: L
Height: 6'2" Weight: 225 Origin: Round 1, 2011 Draft (#43 overall)

YEAR	TEAM	LVL	AGE	W	L	SV	G	GS	IP	H	HR	BB/9	K/9	K	GB%	BABIP
2016	ARI	MLB	26	0	1	0	32	0	22²	22	1	4.4	11.1	28	52%	.368
2017	ARI	MLB	27	1	0	0	71	0	51¹	48	5	3.7	10.7	61	58%	.326
2018	ARI	MLB	28	1	6	0	77	0	49¹	41	0	4.6	9.7	53	51%	.313
2019	ARI	MLB	29	2	2	0	46	0	48	40	4	4.5	9.9	53	50%	.290

Breakout: 28% Improve: 56% Collapse: 23% Attrition: 21% MLB: 93%
Comparables: Alex Colome, Justin Wilson, Zack Britton

Chafin is weird. Sure, he rocked a nasty mustache for much of 2018, once lived in a trailer behind Chase Field and he has a cow-milking title to his name, but he's weird on the mound, too. Chafin ran another good ERA, but it was a bit misleading. He struggled to limit inherited runners from scoring and walked a bunch of guys. He wasn't used as a LOOGY and lefties actually performed better against him than righties did. But he did something else weird: he made 77 appearances without allowing a home run. That's hard to do, even for someone not known for being taken deep. While he surely isn't the most efficient, Chafin has also avoided burning things down and that should keep him in the bullpen mix moving forward.

YEAR	TEAM	LVL	AGE	WHIP	ERA	DRA	WARP	MPH	FB%	WHF	CSP
2016	ARI	MLB	26	1.46	6.75	5.65	-0.2	96.0	72	15.6	47
2017	ARI	MLB	27	1.34	3.51	3.51	0.9	95.1	61.2	11.9	41.8
2018	ARI	MLB	28	1.34	3.10	4.23	0.4	95.2	56.6	14.7	42.7
2019	ARI	MLB	29	1.32	3.66	4.07	0.4	94.6	60.2	13.7	43.5

Andrew Chafin, continued

Pitch Shape vs LHH

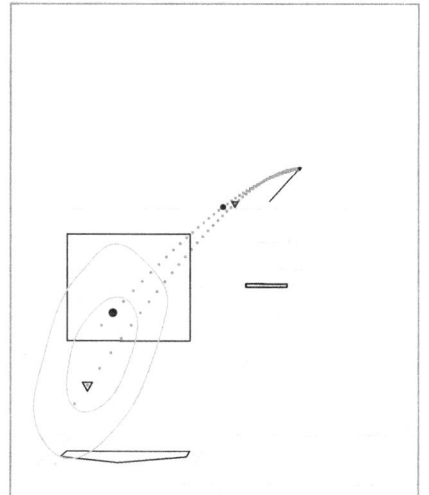

Pitch Shape vs RHH

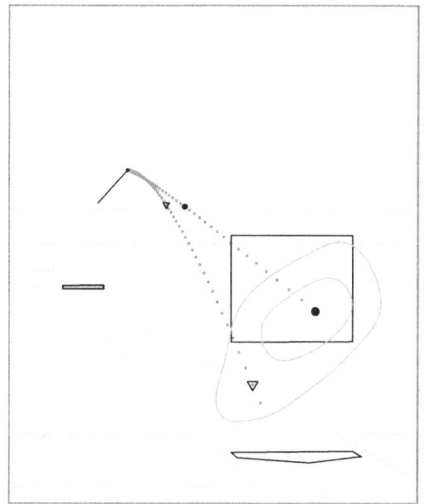

Type	Frequency	Velocity	H Movement	V Movement
● Fastball	56.6%	94 [105]	11.1 [80]	-15.9 [100]
☐ Sinker				
+ Cutter				
▲ Changeup	0.9%	86.5 [105]	10.5 [104]	-21.5 [117]
✕ Splitter				
▽ Slider	42.5%	83.5 [96]	-0.6 [82]	-35.8 [92]
◇ Curveball				
⊕ Slow Curveball				
✳ Knuckleball				
▼ Screwball				

Zack Godley RHP
Born: 04/21/90 Age: 29 Bats: R Throws: R
Height: 6'3" Weight: 240 Origin: Round 10, 2013 Draft (#288 overall)

YEAR	TEAM	LVL	AGE	W	L	SV	G	GS	IP	H	HR	BB/9	K/9	K	GB%	BABIP
2016	MOB	AA	26	2	5	0	8	8	49^1	48	4	2.0	5.7	31	56%	.291
2016	RNO	AAA	26	2	1	0	7	6	32^2	37	3	4.1	10.5	38	50%	.382
2016	ARI	MLB	26	5	4	0	27	9	74^2	86	13	3.0	7.2	60	55%	.313
2017	RNO	AAA	27	2	1	0	5	3	28	14	0	5.5	9.3	29	68%	.222
2017	ARI	MLB	27	8	9	0	26	25	155	124	15	3.1	9.6	165	58%	.280
2018	ARI	MLB	28	15	11	0	33	32	178^1	177	16	4.1	9.3	185	50%	.324
2019	ARI	MLB	29	10	9	0	26	26	156	138	15	3.4	9.0	157	51%	.294

Breakout: 25% Improve: 49% Collapse: 15% Attrition: 16% MLB: 91%
Comparables: Christian Friedrich, Aaron Heilman, Jake Arrieta

It's amazing that a pitcher with Godley's stuff took so long to get drafted. He was 23 when he began his professional career, but reached the majors at 25, rushing through the Cubs' and Diamondbacks' systems with the kind of reckless abandon he's known for on the mound. He was a WTF trade target by Dave Stewart, then showed enough in his Diamondbacks debut to prove he belonged. A promotion from the bullpen to the rotation proved fruitful two years ago, but his 2018 was a bit rougher around the edges. He battled his mechanics for most of the season, falling off the mound like a drunken sailor at times. With pitches that have so much movement (a la Trevor Cahill), he struggles to throw strikes even when he's right, and when he's not, well, that's what 2018 was: too many walks, too many mistakes. Godley competes his ass off every time he takes the mound, but there's plenty of cleaning up to do before he can sparkle again.

YEAR	TEAM	LVL	AGE	WHIP	ERA	DRA	WARP	MPH	FB%	WHF	CSP
2016	MOB	AA	26	1.20	3.83	3.65	0.9				
2016	RNO	AAA	26	1.59	3.31	3.80	0.6				
2016	ARI	MLB	26	1.49	6.39	4.34	0.8	92.8	64.4	12.7	44.3
2017	RNO	AAA	27	1.11	2.57	3.69	0.6				
2017	ARI	MLB	27	1.14	3.37	3.69	3.3	93.0	56.9	13.7	42.3
2018	ARI	MLB	28	1.45	4.74	4.78	1.1	91.5	54.4	12.2	43.4
2019	ARI	MLB	29	1.26	3.66	4.04	1.9	91.6	56.5	12.7	43.2

Zack Godley, continued

Pitch Shape vs LHH

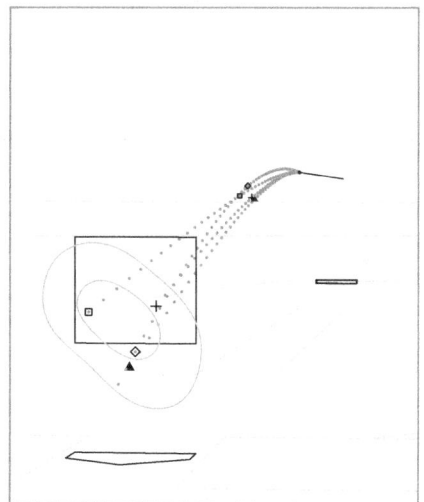

Pitch Shape vs RHH

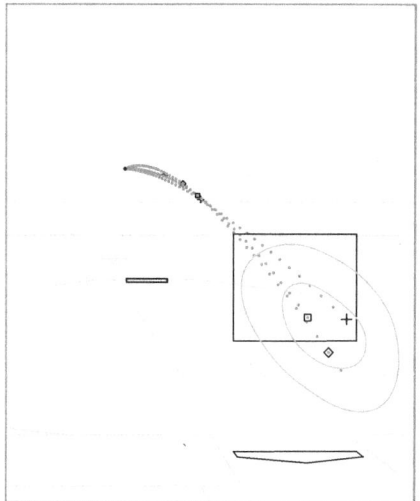

Type	Frequency	Velocity	H Movement	V Movement
● Fastball				
☐ Sinker	32.1%	90.3 [89]	-12.8 [99]	-25.1 [84]
+ Cutter	22.3%	89.3 [103]	-0.9 [84]	-21.9 [107]
▲ Changeup	5.3%	81.5 [85]	-6.8 [124]	-35.2 [77]
✕ Splitter				
▽ Slider				
◇ Curveball	40.3%	81.9 [113]	3.4 [81]	-44.8 [107]
⊕ Slow Curveball				
✱ Knuckleball				
▼ Screwball				

Arizona Diamondbacks 2019

Zack Greinke   RHP
Born: 10/21/83   Age: 35   Bats: R   Throws: R
Height: 6'2"   Weight: 200   Origin: Round 1, 2002 Draft (#6 overall)

YEAR	TEAM	LVL	AGE	W	L	SV	G	GS	IP	H	HR	BB/9	K/9	K	GB%	BABIP
2016	ARI	MLB	32	13	7	0	26	26	158^2	161	23	2.3	7.6	134	47%	.294
2017	ARI	MLB	33	17	7	0	32	32	202^1	172	25	2.0	9.6	215	48%	.285
2018	ARI	MLB	34	15	11	0	33	33	207^2	181	28	1.9	8.6	199	46%	.272
2019	*ARI*	*MLB*	*35*	*12*	*10*	*0*	*29*	*29*	*194^1*	*169*	*22*	*2.3*	*8.7*	*189*	*46%*	*.282*

Breakout: 17%   Improve: 39%   Collapse: 33%   Attrition: 8%   MLB: 90%
Comparables: Adam Wainwright, Bert Blyleven, Hiroki Kuroda

Greinke sat 94-95 mph and flirted with triple digits. A *decade* ago. While his velocity has dropped off in a major way in recent years, his strikeout rate has increased along the way. Greinke has leaned into that decline, as he used his slow curveball, which many have called an "eephus," more than ever in 2018. It's all smoke and mirrors these days for the former Cy Young winner and everybody knows it. While he was less ace-like in the season that was, it appears he's still on track to be a very good pitcher for years to come. His contract is surely burdensome, but he's maintained a productive pace into his mid-30s, defying Father Time in the process.

YEAR	TEAM	LVL	AGE	WHIP	ERA	DRA	WARP	MPH	FB%	WHF	CSP
2016	ARI	MLB	32	1.27	4.37	4.23	2.1	93.8	48.3	11.2	43.1
2017	ARI	MLB	33	1.07	3.20	2.77	6.3	92.3	48.4	13.4	40.9
2018	ARI	MLB	34	1.08	3.21	3.09	5.3	91.4	48.7	11.7	45.1
2019	*ARI*	*MLB*	*35*	*1.12*	*3.61*	*3.98*	*2.4*	*91.0*	*47.6*	*12*	*42.4*

Zack Greinke, continued

Pitch Shape vs LHH

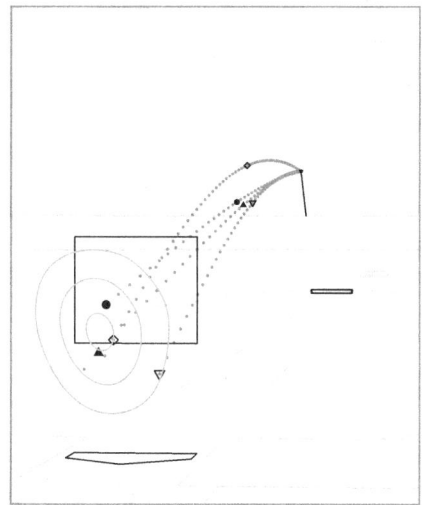

Pitch Shape vs RHH

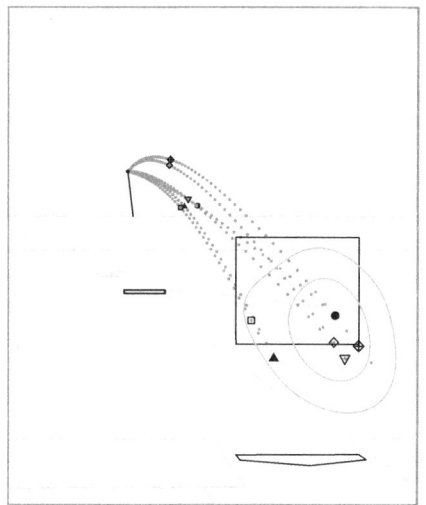

Type	Frequency	Velocity	H Movement	V Movement
● Fastball	43.2%	90 [92]	-0.8 [127]	-15.2 [102]
□ Sinker	5.5%	90.6 [91]	-10.2 [120]	-18.7 [105]
+ Cutter				
▲ Changeup	20.8%	87 [107]	-10.1 [106]	-28.6 [96]
× Splitter				
▽ Slider	17.1%	83.8 [97]	6.6 [107]	-32.6 [101]
◇ Curveball	11.6%	71.3 [73]	10.7 [112]	-59 [75]
⊕ Slow Curveball	1.8%	68 [101]	11.2 [102]	-64.4 [102]
✳ Knuckleball				
▼ Screwball				

Arizona Diamondbacks 2019

Yoshihisa Hirano RHP

Born: 03/08/84   Age: 35   Bats: R   Throws: R
Height: 6'1"   Weight: 185   Origin: International Free Agent, 2017

YEAR	TEAM	LVL	AGE	W	L	SV	G	GS	IP	H	HR	BB/9	K/9	K	GB%	BABIP
2018	ARI	MLB	34	4	3	3	75	0	66.1	49	6	3.1	8.0	59	51%	.250
2019	ARI	MLB	35	3	3	8	51	0	53	49	6	3.8	8.2	49	49%	.291

Breakout: 24%   Improve: 51%   Collapse: 20%   Attrition: 17%   MLB: 88%
Comparables: Trever Miller, Hideki Okajima, Mike Stanton

Is magic real or is it just a trick to make the kids question reality? For non-believers, magic seems frivolous. For those who choose to accept the bounds of magic, anything is possible. For the Diamondbacks faithful, Hirano convinced many that magic is indeed alive and well among us. His splitter has Houdini-like properties and batters swung and missed at nearly 20 percent of them. His mediocre fastball was very real — almost too real — but the splitter was simply magic. Even if hitters managed to make contact, they routinely pounded it into the ground. While the profile is not closer-esque, he may find himself back in the closer conversation in 2019.

YEAR	TEAM	LVL	AGE	WHIP	ERA	DRA	WARP	MPH	FB%	WHF	CSP
2018	ARI	MLB	34	1.09	2.44	4.47	0.3	93.3	53.7	13.5	42.4
2019	ARI	MLB	35	1.33	4.08	4.44	0.2	92.1	52.7	13.2	41.6

Yoshihisa Hirano, continued

Pitch Shape vs LHH

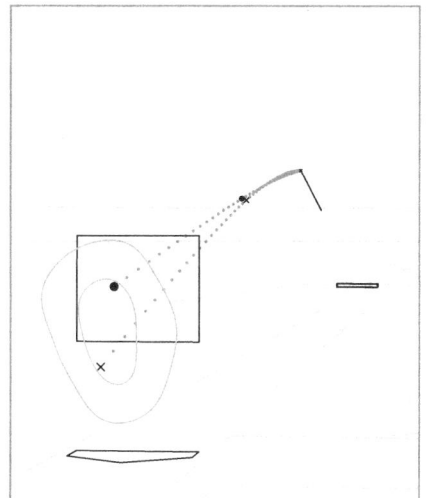

Pitch Shape vs RHH

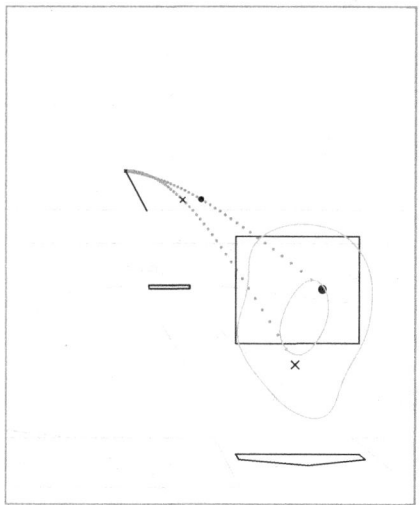

Type	Frequency	Velocity	H Movement	V Movement
● Fastball	53.7%	91.9 [98]	-7.4 [97]	-13.9 [106]
□ Sinker				
+ Cutter				
▲ Changeup				
× Splitter	46.3%	83.8 [90]	-6.4 [107]	-33.1 [85]
▽ Slider				
◇ Curveball				
✦ Slow Curveball				
✳ Knuckleball				
▼ Screwball				

Arizona Diamondbacks 2019

Greg Holland   RHP
Born: 11/20/85   Age: 33   Bats: R   Throws: R
Height: 5'10"   Weight: 205   Origin: Round 10, 2007 Draft (#306 overall)

YEAR	TEAM	LVL	AGE	W	L	SV	G	GS	IP	H	HR	BB/9	K/9	K	GB%	BABIP
2017	COL	MLB	31	3	6	41	61	0	57^1	40	7	4.1	11.0	70	41%	.252
2018	SLN	MLB	32	0	2	0	32	0	25	34	1	7.9	7.9	22	39%	.379
2018	WAS	MLB	32	2	0	3	24	0	21^1	9	1	4.2	10.5	25	50%	.186
2019	ARI	MLB	33	3	3	14	51	0	53	49	7	5.0	9.1	54	41%	.293

Breakout: 17%   Improve: 41%   Collapse: 33%   Attrition: 9%   MLB: 92%
Comparables: Fernando Rodney, Pedro Strop, Damaso Marte

The Cardinals gave him $14 million and he gave them a 7.92 ERA in 25 stomach-sinking innings. With Washington, though, Holland turned in 21 innings of a 0.84 ERA to finish out the year. He lives in the low-to-mid-90s now — the 96-plus velocity just isn't coming back — and he may still be adjusting to it. His curveball usage spiked once he got to D.C., and either with it or just by coincidence, so did his ground-ball rate. Having seen such a dramatic shift in the middle of a season, it's worth noting that his DRA numbers totally lined up with the horrific St. Louis ERA and seemed to support the idea of his Washington improvements (within reason).

YEAR	TEAM	LVL	AGE	WHIP	ERA	DRA	WARP	MPH	FB%	WHF	CSP
2017	COL	MLB	31	1.15	3.61	3.58	1.0	95.3	44.4	15.7	47
2018	SLN	MLB	32	2.24	7.92	6.77	-0.5	94.5	43	12.4	43.1
2018	WAS	MLB	32	0.89	0.84	3.77	0.3	94.4	44.2	16.4	40.9
2019	ARI	MLB	33	1.47	4.72	4.93	-0.1	93.8	43.4	14.6	43.8

Greg Holland, continued

Pitch Shape vs LHH

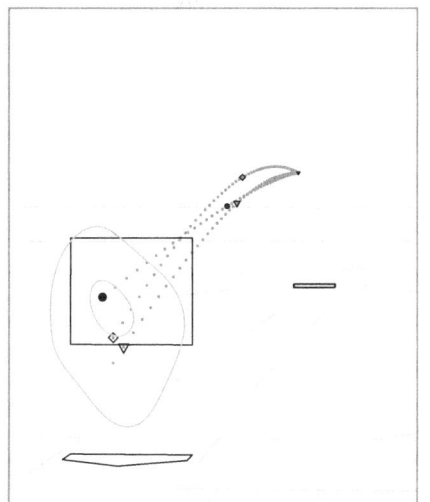

Pitch Shape vs RHH

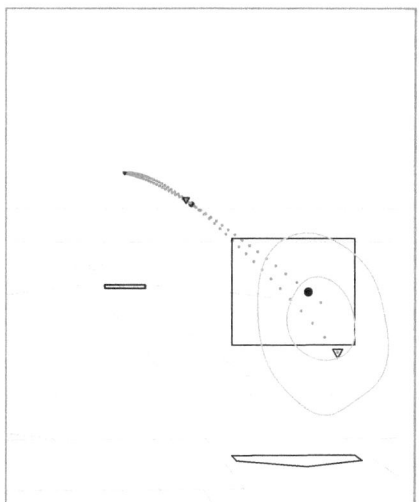

Type	Frequency	Velocity	H Movement	V Movement
● Fastball	43.5%	93.4 [103]	-0.3 [130]	-13.4 [107]
□ Sinker				
+ Cutter				
▲ Changeup				
× Splitter	0.1%	87.4 [110]	-8.5 [99]	-26.1 [114]
▽ Slider	45.3%	86.7 [110]	4.8 [100]	-30.6 [107]
◇ Curveball	11.1%	78.8 [101]	5 [88]	-47.7 [101]
⊕ Slow Curveball				
✳ Knuckleball				
▼ Screwball				

Arizona Diamondbacks 2019

Matthew Koch RHP
Born: 11/02/90 Age: 28 Bats: L Throws: R
Height: 6'3" Weight: 215 Origin: Round 3, 2012 Draft (#107 overall)

YEAR	TEAM	LVL	AGE	W	L	SV	G	GS	IP	H	HR	BB/9	K/9	K	GB%	BABIP
2016	MOB	AA	25	2	4	0	14	14	74²	87	7	1.6	5.9	49	42%	.324
2016	RNO	AAA	25	4	2	0	7	7	46²	55	3	1.2	4.8	25	55%	.325
2016	ARI	MLB	25	1	1	1	7	2	18	9	1	2.0	5.0	10	43%	.154
2017	YAK	A-	26	1	0	0	2	2	11	13	2	0.8	7.4	9	41%	.344
2017	ARI	MLB	26	0	0	0	1	0	0	2	0			0	0%	1.000
2017	RNO	AAA	26	2	2	0	10	10	45	68	11	3.0	5.0	25	45%	.350
2018	RNO	AAA	27	2	4	0	11	11	54¹	66	11	2.0	5.1	31	46%	.312
2018	ARI	MLB	27	5	5	0	19	14	86²	88	19	2.3	5.2	50	45%	.262
2019	ARI	MLB	28	4	5	0	38	8	74	81	13	3.0	6.0	50	44%	.294

Breakout: 7%   Improve: 18%   Collapse: 12%   Attrition: 22%   MLB: 36%
Comparables: Josh Geer, Pat Dean, Christian Bergman

Every kid plays with fire. Maybe it's hardwired into humans as part of our Neanderthal past. Maybe it's just stupid fascination and a resistance to being told not to do something. Either way, if you play with fire you'll get burned at some point and Koch did just that in 2018. It's hard to make your living as pitcher surrendering a lot of contact and Koch has no way around it. His stuff is just too hittable. Working as an up-and-down option for the Diamondbacks, things were more down than up in the majors, where he was mostly torched. He started hot but an unsustainable BABIP didn't hold and the rest went up in flames.

YEAR	TEAM	LVL	AGE	WHIP	ERA	DRA	WARP	MPH	FB%	WHF	CSP
2016	MOB	AA	25	1.34	4.70	4.31	0.7				
2016	RNO	AAA	25	1.31	3.09	4.80	0.3				
2016	ARI	MLB	25	0.72	2.00	6.36	-0.2	94.2	49.6	9	53.1
2017	YAK	A-	26	1.27	4.91	4.92	0.0				
2017	ARI	MLB	26					91.9	55.6	0	57
2017	RNO	AAA	26	1.84	8.40	8.81	-1.5				
2018	RNO	AAA	27	1.44	5.96	5.47	0.1				
2018	ARI	MLB	27	1.27	4.15	5.80	-0.5	93.0	41.1	7.6	49.1
2019	ARI	MLB	28	1.42	5.37	5.67	-0.6	92.6	42.2	7.7	53.1

Matthew Koch, continued

Pitch Shape vs LHH

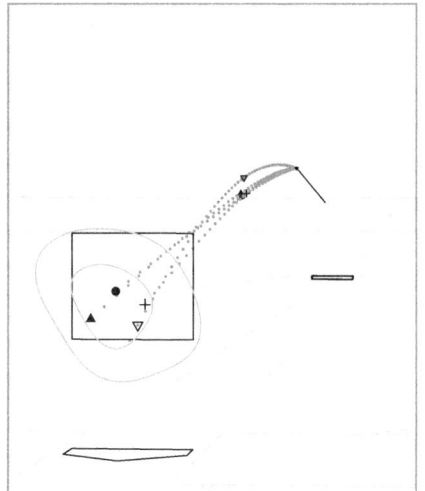

Pitch Shape vs RHH

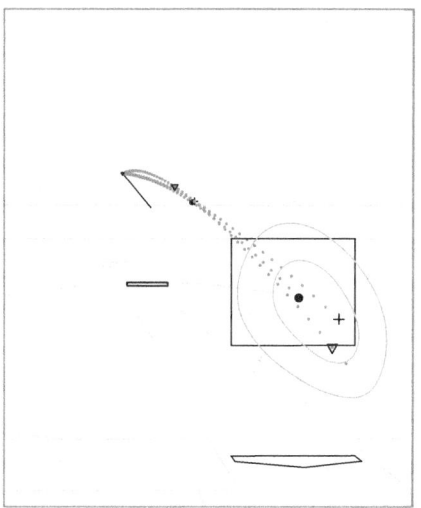

Type	Frequency	Velocity	H Movement	V Movement
● Fastball	41.0%	91.8 [98]	-9.7 [86]	-16.2 [99]
☐ Sinker				
+ Cutter	26.8%	90.2 [108]	-0.3 [87]	-21.9 [107]
▲ Changeup	16.5%	85.9 [102]	-10.3 [105]	-25.2 [106]
✕ Splitter				
▽ Slider	14.9%	80.2 [81]	8.7 [117]	-41.4 [75]
◇ Curveball	0.8%	79.3 [103]	8.2 [102]	-42.9 [112]
✦ Slow Curveball				
✳ Knuckleball				
▼ Screwball				

T.J. McFarland LHP
Born: 06/08/89 Age: 30 Bats: L Throws: L
Height: 6'3" Weight: 220 Origin: Round 4, 2007 Draft (#137 overall)

YEAR	TEAM	LVL	AGE	W	L	SV	G	GS	IP	H	HR	BB/9	K/9	K	GB%	BABIP
2016	BAL	MLB	27	2	2	0	16	0	24²	33	3	3.6	2.6	7	60%	.333
2016	NOR	AAA	27	1	1	0	8	4	26¹	33	3	2.4	3.8	11	63%	.330
2017	RNO	AAA	28	0	0	1	7	0	11	6	0	3.3	7.4	9	81%	.231
2017	ARI	MLB	28	4	5	0	43	1	54	65	4	2.8	4.8	29	69%	.323
2018	ARI	MLB	29	2	2	1	47	0	72	64	4	2.8	5.2	42	68%	.268
2019	ARI	MLB	30	3	3	0	51	0	53	56	5	3.8	6.1	36	59%	.299

Breakout: 28% Improve: 53% Collapse: 21% Attrition: 12% MLB: 84%
Comparables: Sam Dyson, Jared Hughes, Brad Ziegler

Strangers waiting up and down the boulevard, their shadows searching in the night. Streetlights, people, living just to find emotion, hiding somewhere in the night. Presumably, many stopped believing in McFarland quite some time ago. Once a first-round draft pick by the Orioles, the journeyman has found some kind of niche as an effective long reliever. His skill isn't limited to garbage innings, either. He's a low-90s lefty sinkerballer who won't miss any bats but doesn't walk anyone while inducing a boatload of ground balls — nearly 70 percent in 2018. He keeps the ball in the yard and lets his defense do the work. McFarland might have even pitched his way into consideration for a higher-leverage role in 2019.

YEAR	TEAM	LVL	AGE	WHIP	ERA	DRA	WARP	MPH	FB%	WHF	CSP
2016	BAL	MLB	27	1.74	6.93	6.79	-0.5	93.9	68.6	6.2	44.3
2016	NOR	AAA	27	1.52	4.44	4.38	0.3				
2017	RNO	AAA	28	0.91	0.00	3.54	0.2				
2017	ARI	MLB	28	1.52	5.33	5.89	-0.4	92.6	73.1	7.7	43.7
2018	ARI	MLB	29	1.19	2.00	4.72	0.2	91.9	72.7	8.8	41.6
2019	ARI	MLB	30	1.46	4.48	4.76	0.0	91.6	72.1	8.1	42.8

T.J. McFarland, continued

Pitch Shape vs LHH

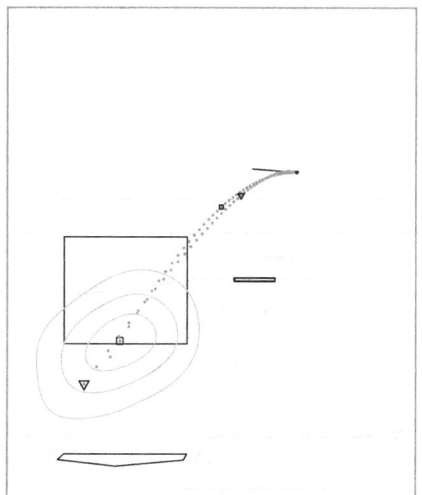

Pitch Shape vs RHH

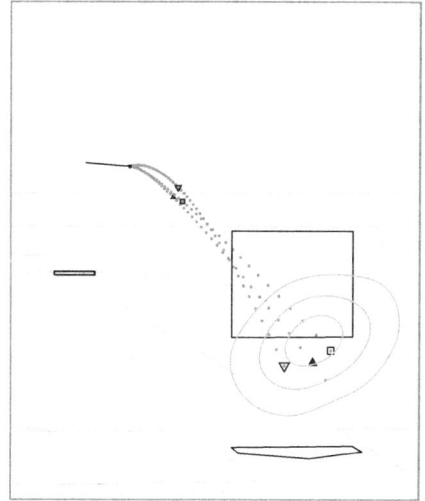

Type	Frequency	Velocity	H Movement	V Movement
● Fastball	0.1%	90.4 [93]	7.1 [98]	-19.1 [89]
□ Sinker	72.6%	91 [93]	15.6 [75]	-27.8 [76]
+ Cutter				
▲ Changeup	13.4%	83.7 [93]	14.3 [84]	-33.1 [83]
× Splitter				
▽ Slider	14.0%	80.5 [82]	-5.4 [102]	-40.7 [77]
◇ Curveball				
⊕ Slow Curveball				
✳ Knuckleball				
▼ Screwball				

Arizona Diamondbacks 2019

Robbie Ray LHP
Born: 10/01/91 Age: 27 Bats: L Throws: L
Height: 6'2" Weight: 195 Origin: Round 12, 2010 Draft (#356 overall)

YEAR	TEAM	LVL	AGE	W	L	SV	G	GS	IP	H	HR	BB/9	K/9	K	GB%	BABIP
2016	ARI	MLB	24	8	15	0	32	32	174^1	185	24	3.7	11.3	218	47%	.352
2017	ARI	MLB	25	15	5	0	28	28	162	116	23	3.9	12.1	218	42%	.267
2018	ARI	MLB	26	6	2	0	24	24	123^2	97	19	5.1	12.0	165	41%	.292
2019	ARI	MLB	27	9	8	0	26	26	137	110	13	4.0	11.4	174	42%	.299

Breakout: 33% Improve: 67% Collapse: 15% Attrition: 9% MLB: 95%
Comparables: Max Scherzer, Jonathan Sanchez, Brandon Morrow

Make no mistake, Ray's 2018 was not exactly what he and the Diamondbacks were hoping for. But another thing remains true: the lefty has come a long way. His season got off to a rocky start when he was shelled in Colorado early and his results bounced around for a bit thereafter. An oblique injury put him on the shelf, but he was better upon his return. During his last eight starts, he allowed just 2.31 runs per nine innings and struck out 61. He was tough to hit, but he continued walking more than his share. Still, the emerging lefty was able to buckle down and get the strikeouts needed, *when he needed them*, to post much better results. On the surface, Ray's season looks like a disappointment, but he finished it with a prolonged stretch of dominance that may propel him into 2019 as an excellent bounce-back candidate.

YEAR	TEAM	LVL	AGE	WHIP	ERA	DRA	WARP	MPH	FB%	WHF	CSP
2016	ARI	MLB	24	1.47	4.90	4.22	2.3	97.2	71.3	12.4	47.2
2017	ARI	MLB	25	1.15	2.89	3.06	4.6	96.3	59.3	15.3	44.2
2018	ARI	MLB	26	1.35	3.93	3.99	1.9	96.0	53.9	13.8	44.8
2019	ARI	MLB	27	1.25	3.29	3.62	2.3	96.0	61.7	14.1	45.7

Robbie Ray, continued

Pitch Shape vs LHH

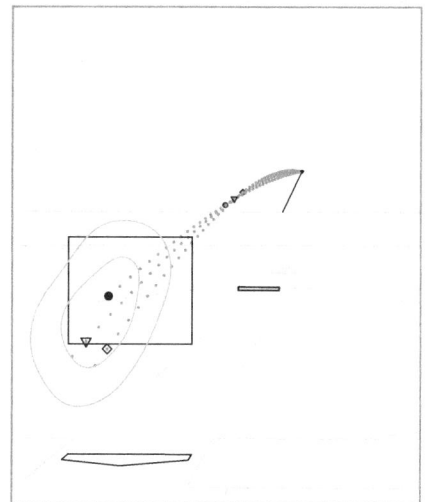

Pitch Shape vs RHH

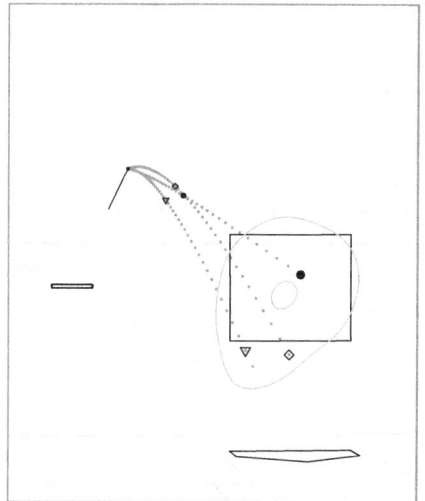

Type	Frequency	Velocity	H Movement	V Movement
● Fastball	53.5%	94.1 [105]	8.2 [93]	-12.6 [110]
☐ Sinker	0.5%	93.8 [107]	11 [114]	-14.6 [119]
+ Cutter				
▲ Changeup				
× Splitter				
▽ Slider	25.7%	85 [102]	-0.5 [81]	-30 [109]
◇ Curveball	20.4%	83 [117]	-0.8 [70]	-39.7 [119]
⊕ Slow Curveball				
✳ Knuckleball				
▼ Screwball				

Jimmie Sherfy RHP
Born: 12/27/91   Age: 27   Bats: R   Throws: R
Height: 6'0"   Weight: 175   Origin: Round 10, 2013 Draft (#300 overall)

YEAR	TEAM	LVL	AGE	W	L	SV	G	GS	IP	H	HR	BB/9	K/9	K	GB%	BABIP
2016	VIS	A+	24	0	0	8	12	0	12^1	5	0	4.4	15.3	21	68%	.263
2016	MOB	AA	24	2	0	10	16	0	19^2	6	1	2.3	14.2	31	51%	.147
2016	RNO	AAA	24	1	4	12	24	0	23^1	20	5	5.0	10.4	27	42%	.288
2017	RNO	AAA	25	2	1	20	44	0	49	37	6	1.8	11.2	61	35%	.279
2017	ARI	MLB	25	2	0	1	11	0	10^2	5	0	1.7	7.6	9	54%	.192
2018	RNO	AAA	26	5	1	15	38	0	45	31	1	4.0	11.6	58	36%	.283
2018	ARI	MLB	26	0	0	0	15	0	16^1	8	1	5.5	9.4	17	40%	.179
2019	ARI	MLB	27	2	2	0	30	0	32	27	4	4.3	10.1	36	40%	.290

Breakout: 12%   Improve: 29%   Collapse: 29%   Attrition: 22%   MLB: 63%
Comparables: Cory Gearrin, Blake Parker, Spencer Patton

It's hard to call relievers prospects. Most were prospects at some point when they were, usually, starting pitchers. But those relief-only guys are tough. Sherfy was once an exception to the rule because, a) he was quite good, and b) the Diamondbacks' farm system was really quite bad. Entering his age-27 season, Sherfy is a prospect no more, yet the Diamondbacks' faithful are still looking forward to seeing him truly get his chance. The funkiness in his delivery has been toned down in an effort to throw more strikes, but the results remain a work in progress. Arizona will always covet inexpensive relievers with minor-league options and Sherfy fits in that regard.

YEAR	TEAM	LVL	AGE	WHIP	ERA	DRA	WARP	MPH	FB%	WHF	CSP
2016	VIS	A+	24	0.89	0.00	1.36	0.5				
2016	MOB	AA	24	0.56	0.46	1.38	0.8				
2016	RNO	AAA	24	1.41	6.17	3.74	0.3				
2017	RNO	AAA	25	0.96	3.12	3.21	1.1				
2017	ARI	MLB	25	0.66	0.00	6.00	-0.1	95.5	46.8	7.7	43.9
2018	RNO	AAA	26	1.13	1.60	2.75	1.2				
2018	ARI	MLB	26	1.10	1.65	6.54	-0.3	95.4	46.5	10.1	39.7
2019	ARI	MLB	27	1.33	4.32	4.62	0.1	95.0	47.1	9.5	42.1

Jimmie Sherfy, continued

Pitch Shape vs LHH

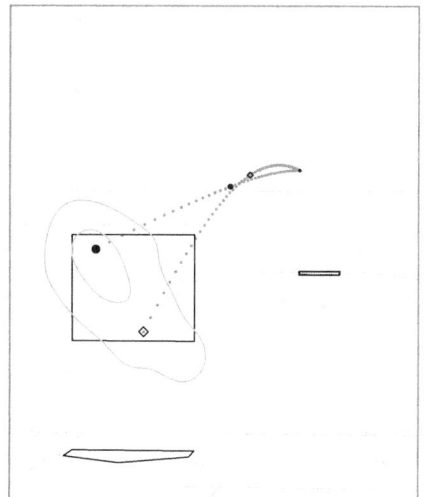

Pitch Shape vs RHH

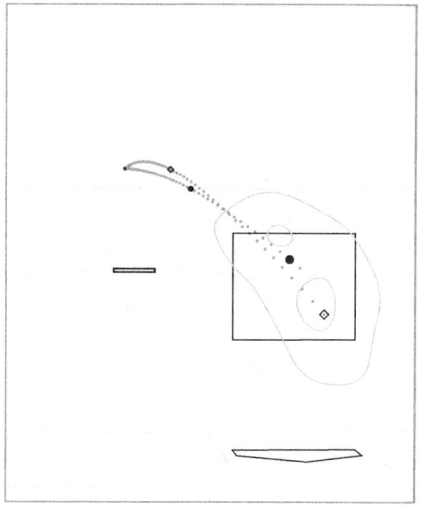

Type	Frequency	Velocity	H Movement	V Movement
● Fastball	46.5%	93.7 [104]	-5.8 [104]	-14.1 [105]
☐ Sinker				
+ Cutter				
▲ Changeup	4.9%	83 [91]	-9.8 [108]	-29.6 [93]
✕ Splitter				
▽ Slider	5.2%	80.2 [81]	10.2 [123]	-41.7 [74]
◇ Curveball	43.4%	77.6 [97]	9.4 [107]	-44.2 [109]
⊕ Slow Curveball				
✳ Knuckleball				
▼ Screwball				

Taijuan Walker RHP
Born: 08/13/92   Age: 26   Bats: R   Throws: R
Height: 6'4"   Weight: 235   Origin: Round 1, 2010 Draft (#43 overall)

YEAR	TEAM	LVL	AGE	W	L	SV	G	GS	IP	H	HR	BB/9	K/9	K	GB%	BABIP
2016	TAC	AAA	23	1	0	0	3	3	15	12	1	4.8	3.6	6	55%	.220
2016	SEA	MLB	23	8	11	0	25	25	134^1	129	27	2.5	8.0	119	45%	.267
2017	ARI	MLB	24	9	9	0	28	28	157^1	148	17	3.5	8.4	146	50%	.291
2018	ARI	MLB	25	0	0	0	3	3	13	15	1	3.5	6.2	9	45%	.341
2019	ARI	MLB	26	4	5	0	13	13	65	62	8	3.4	8.0	58	45%	.289

Breakout: 18%   Improve: 50%   Collapse: 17%   Attrition: 13%   MLB: 99%
Comparables: John Danks, Julio Teheran, Johnny Cueto

When the Diamondbacks traded Jean Segura and Mitch Haniger (and Zac Curtis) to the Mariners for Ketel Marte and Walker, it seemed like the proverbial "challenge trade." Here was a pretty fair exchange of talent, and any gap in that talent was offset by team control and future contracts. The Diamondbacks weren't going to be able to extend Segura, so they let him go in an effort to get back cost-controlled pitching. The risk was always the worry of injury, and while Haniger has missed some time in Seattle, Walker made just three starts in 2018 before his elbow gave. He headed for Tommy John surgery and will rejoin the Diamondbacks around the All-Star break if things go well.

YEAR	TEAM	LVL	AGE	WHIP	ERA	DRA	WARP	MPH	FB%	WHF	CSP
2016	TAC	AAA	23	1.33	3.60	3.60	0.3				
2016	SEA	MLB	23	1.24	4.22	4.53	1.3	97.0	68.1	10.9	46.9
2017	ARI	MLB	24	1.33	3.49	4.90	1.2	95.6	59.1	9.7	46.7
2018	ARI	MLB	25	1.54	3.46	5.15	0.0	96.0	70.5	7.1	53.8
2019	ARI	MLB	26	1.31	4.28	4.70	0.3	95.8	64.2	10.2	50.6

Taijuan Walker, continued

Pitch Shape vs LHH

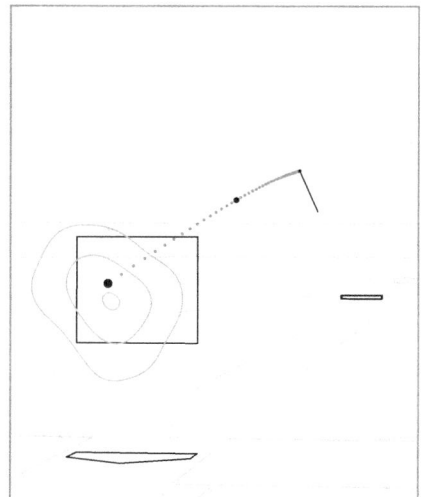

Pitch Shape vs RHH

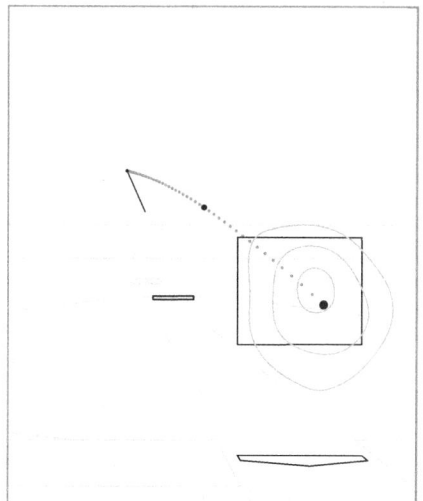

Type	Frequency	Velocity	H Movement	V Movement
● Fastball	69.6%	94.4 [106]	-7.2 [97]	-12.7 [110]
□ Sinker	0.9%	92.4 [100]	-12.4 [102]	-22.1 [94]
+ Cutter				
▲ Changeup				
✕ Splitter	12.5%	89.3 [120]	-11.7 [87]	-23.2 [127]
▽ Slider	8.5%	88.8 [119]	3.2 [93]	-22.6 [131]
◇ Curveball	8.5%	77.3 [96]	10.7 [112]	-51.6 [92]
⊕ Slow Curveball				
✴ Knuckleball				
▼ Screwball				

Luke Weaver RHP

Born: 08/21/93 Age: 25 Bats: R Throws: R
Height: 6'2" Weight: 170 Origin: Round 1, 2014 Draft (#27 overall)

YEAR	TEAM	LVL	AGE	W	L	SV	G	GS	IP	H	HR	BB/9	K/9	K	GB%	BABIP
2016	SFD	AA	22	6	3	0	12	12	77	63	4	1.2	10.3	88	40%	.289
2016	MEM	AAA	22	1	0	0	1	1	6	2	0	3.0	6.0	4	38%	.125
2016	SLN	MLB	22	1	4	0	9	8	36^1	46	7	3.0	11.1	45	37%	.386
2017	MEM	AAA	23	10	2	0	15	15	77^2	63	3	2.2	8.8	76	46%	.291
2017	SLN	MLB	23	7	2	0	13	10	60^1	59	7	2.5	10.7	72	51%	.335
2018	SLN	MLB	24	7	11	0	30	25	136^1	150	19	3.6	8.0	121	44%	.318
2019	ARI	MLB	25	7	7	0	23	23	115	109	13	2.9	9.1	116	42%	.300

Breakout: 30%   Improve: 63%   Collapse: 17%   Attrition: 20%   MLB: 95%
Comparables: Danny Salazar, Patrick Corbin, Jordan Zimmermann

Throwing harder than ever and with some newfound, much-needed separation between his fastball and changeup, Weaver showed why he's such a tantalizing arm, despite the very uneven season. Alas, he still hasn't found a cutter or slider that works, and his curveball just isn't tight enough to consistently fool anyone. Limited mostly to the heater and the change, and persistently wispy on the mound, he looks more and more like a reliever. In that role, however, he could really thrive. It's a live fastball, the changeup comes out of the same slot and he's smart and athletic. If he gets and embraces an opportunity to become a multi-inning fireman, he could prove a very valuable one, but the Diamondbacks figure to give him every opportunity to be an impact starter first.

YEAR	TEAM	LVL	AGE	WHIP	ERA	DRA	WARP	MPH	FB%	WHF	CSP
2016	SFD	AA	22	0.95	1.40	2.70	2.2				
2016	MEM	AAA	22	0.67	0.00	3.17	0.1				
2016	SLN	MLB	22	1.60	5.70	4.40	0.4	94.9	60	10.3	47.2
2017	MEM	AAA	23	1.06	2.55	2.60	2.6				
2017	SLN	MLB	23	1.26	3.88	3.19	1.6	95.5	60.2	10.8	50
2018	SLN	MLB	24	1.50	4.95	4.62	1.1	95.7	57.7	10.4	48.9
2019	ARI	MLB	25	1.28	3.72	4.10	1.3	95.3	59.9	10.7	50

Luke Weaver, continued

Pitch Shape vs LHH

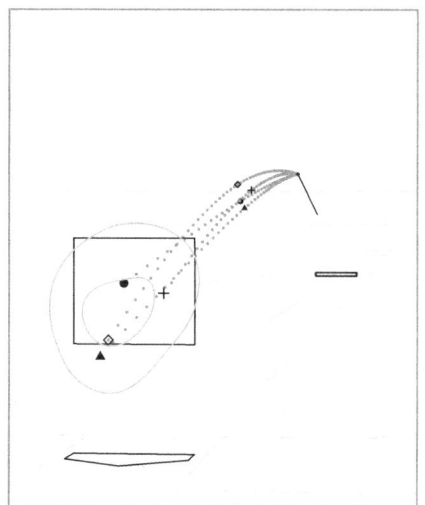

Pitch Shape vs RHH

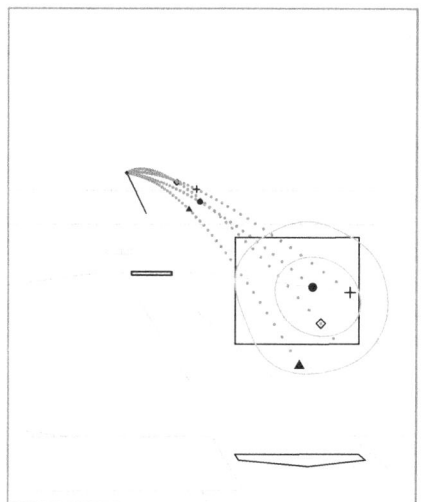

Type	Frequency	Velocity	H Movement	V Movement
● Fastball	56.4%	94.3 [106]	-6.9 [99]	-13.5 [107]
□ Sinker	1.2%	93.2 [104]	-11.3 [111]	-16.7 [112]
+ Cutter	4.8%	87.4 [92]	2.7 [105]	-24.8 [96]
▲ Changeup	24.8%	85.9 [102]	-10.2 [106]	-25.8 [104]
× Splitter				
▽ Slider				
◇ Curveball	12.7%	81.3 [111]	8 [101]	-40.7 [116]
⊕ Slow Curveball				
✳ Knuckleball				
▼ Screwball				

Arizona Diamondbacks 2019

Jazz Chisholm SS
Born: 02/01/98   Age: 21   Bats: L   Throws: R
Height: 5'11"   Weight: 165   Origin: International Free Agent, 2015

YEAR	TEAM	LVL	AGE	PA	R	2B	3B	HR	RBI	BB	K	SB	CS	AVG/OBP/SLG
2016	MSO	RK	18	270	42	12	1	9	37	19	73	13	4	.281/.333/.446
2017	KNC	A	19	125	14	5	2	1	12	10	39	3	0	.248/.325/.358
2018	KNC	A	20	341	52	17	4	15	43	30	97	8	2	.244/.311/.472
2018	VIS	A+	20	160	27	6	2	10	27	9	52	9	2	.329/.369/.597
2019	ARI	MLB	21	251	25	6	1	8	23	9	94	3	1	.163/.193/.297

Breakout: 6%   Improve: 11%   Collapse: 1%   Attrition: 8%   MLB: 12%
Comparables: Trevor Story, Joel Guzman, Javier Guerra

Thelonious Monk once said, "You've got to dig it to dig it, you dig?" In Chisholm's case, most dig. There aren't many 20-year-olds jamming out 25 dingers. There are even fewer of them with the sweet, smooth actions to jive at shortstop. Chisholm missed much of the 2017 campaign with a knee injury, but returned in 2018 to do some serious damage. While his overall line wasn't great, he put the bass in baseball by making the most of his batted balls, especially once he reached Visalia. He's growing in his approach and admitted to trying too hard at times in Kane County. Jazz is supposed be a natural expression and Chisholm is still learning to let the game come to him. If the approach comes together, his crescendo could be transcendent.

YEAR	TEAM	LVL	AGE	PA	DRC+	VORP	BABIP	BRR	FRAA	WARP
2016	MSO	RK	18	270	81	15.4	.363	0.6	SS(60): 2.5, 2B(1): 0.0	0.3
2017	KNC	A	19	125	93	6.4	.371	0.7	SS(29): 0.8	0.4
2018	KNC	A	20	341	101	17.7	.303	-1.4	SS(75): -0.3	0.9
2018	VIS	A+	20	160	139	21.0	.443	0.5	SS(36): -0.7	0.9
2019	ARI	MLB	21	251	25	-12.8	.220	0.2	SS 1	-1.3

Carson Kelly C

Born: 07/14/94 Age: 24 Bats: R Throws: R
Height: 6'2" Weight: 220 Origin: Round 2, 2012 Draft (#86 overall)

YEAR	TEAM	LVL	AGE	PA	R	2B	3B	HR	RBI	BB	K	SB	CS	AVG/OBP/SLG
2016	SFD	AA	21	236	29	7	0	6	18	14	46	0	1	.287/.338/.403
2016	MEM	AAA	21	126	14	10	0	0	14	11	17	0	0	.292/.352/.381
2016	SLN	MLB	21	14	1	1	0	0	1	0	2	0	0	.154/.214/.231
2017	MEM	AAA	22	280	37	13	0	10	41	33	40	0	2	.283/.375/.459
2017	SLN	MLB	22	75	5	3	0	0	6	5	11	0	0	.174/.240/.217
2018	MEM	AAA	23	349	38	14	1	7	41	48	48	0	0	.269/.378/.395
2018	SLN	MLB	23	42	1	0	0	0	3	3	7	0	0	.114/.205/.114
2019	ARI	MLB	24	364	41	15	2	11	42	33	69	0	0	.257/.331/.418

Breakout: 15% Improve: 37% Collapse: 2% Attrition: 20% MLB: 56%
Comparables: Josh Thole, Christian Vazquez, Victor Caratini

Kelly's long-term evaluation comes down to whether you believe in the long arc and late acceleration of catcher development. He's played seven pro seasons, five of them since making the transition from third base to catcher, and he's had offensive success only when seeing a league for a second time. He's gone sideways as a receiver, rather than making any great forward leap. In three tastes of the big leagues, he's looked utterly overmatched at the plate and just okay behind it. Pushing against all those red flags are the hit tool scouts have liked since he was in high school, an exceptionally polished approach and the fact that he's still just 24, at a position where 24 isn't all that old for a prospect.

YEAR	TEAM	P. COUNT	FRM RUNS	BLK RUNS	THRW RUNS	TOT RUNS
2016	SLN	539	-0.2	0.2	0.0	0.2
2017	MEM	9388	11.5	1.2	-0.1	12.2
2017	SLN	2565	2.5	0.4	0.1	3.2
2018	MEM	11582	9.0	0.5	0.7	9.9
2018	SLN	1715	-0.8	-0.3	0.0	-1.1
2019	ARI	12894	4.4	0.9	-0.6	4.7

YEAR	TEAM	LVL	AGE	PA	DRC+	VORP	BABIP	BRR	FRAA	WARP
2016	SFD	AA	21	236	119	14.4	.339	-0.9	C(60): 7.6	1.8
2016	MEM	AAA	21	126	115	5.8	.340	-0.1	C(32): 2.4	0.8
2016	SLN	MLB	21	14	76	-0.4	.182	-0.2	C(10): -0.1	0.0
2017	MEM	AAA	22	280	130	22.1	.304	-1.9	C(68): 10.8	2.9
2017	SLN	MLB	22	75	73	-4.0	.207	0.7	C(31): 3.0	0.5
2018	MEM	AAA	23	349	113	24.7	.299	-0.6	C(83): 10.1, 1B(1): 0.0	2.8
2018	SLN	MLB	23	42	74	-3.2	.143	-0.2	C(16): -0.9	0.0
2019	ARI	MLB	24	364	96	14.5	.288	-0.6	C 2	1.5

Arizona Diamondbacks 2019

Jake McCarthy CF
Born: 07/30/97 Age: 21 Bats: L Throws: L
Height: 6'3" Weight: 195 Origin: Round 1, 2018 Draft (#39 overall)

YEAR	TEAM	LVL	AGE	PA	R	2B	3B	HR	RBI	BB	K	SB	CS	AVG/OBP/SLG
2018	YAK	A-	20	241	33	17	3	3	18	22	40	20	8	.288/.378/.442
2019	ARI	MLB	21	251	28	12	0	6	20	10	66	7	3	.172/.219/.308

Breakout: 1% Improve: 2% Collapse: 0% Attrition: 2% MLB: 2%
Comparables: Abraham Almonte, Xavier Avery, Raimel Tapia

Michael Scott excitedly starts a Willy Wonka-inspired promotion by providing discounts to clients who receive golden tickets, then tries to blame the idea on Dwight Schrute when the promotion appears to cost the company an excessive amount of money. David Wallace comes to the Scranton branch and says the customer was so pleased with the discount they decided to make the company their exclusive provider of office supplies. Grateful, David congratulates Dwight for the idea and, after a moment's hesitation, Dwight accepts the credit. Michael is shocked and upset. McCarthy, a Scranton native, watches it all unravel from the outfield grass where he, and the Diamondbacks, hope he becomes a golden ticket in his own right.

YEAR	TEAM	LVL	AGE	PA	DRC+	VORP	BABIP	BRR	FRAA	WARP
2018	YAK	A-	20	241	143	20.3	.341	-0.5	CF(44): 8.0, LF(11): -2.3	1.5
2019	ARI	MLB	21	251	38	-9.2	.209	0.4	CF 3, LF 0	-0.7

Geraldo Perdomo SS

Born: 10/22/99 Age: 19 Bats: B Throws: R
Height: 6'2" Weight: 184 Origin: International Free Agent, 2016

YEAR	TEAM	LVL	AGE	PA	R	2B	3B	HR	RBI	BB	K	SB	CS	AVG/OBP/SLG
2017	DDI	RK	17	278	42	3	2	1	11	60	37	16	8	.238/.410/.285
2018	DIA	RK	18	101	20	4	2	1	8	14	17	14	1	.314/.416/.442
2018	MSO	RK	18	29	3	0	1	0	2	7	4	1	1	.455/.586/.545
2018	YAK	A-	18	127	20	3	2	3	14	18	23	9	4	.301/.421/.456
2019	ARI	MLB	19	251	26	0	0	6	17	24	70	5	2	.138/.220/.213

Breakout: 11% Improve: 13% Collapse: 0% Attrition: 9% MLB: 15%
Comparables: Gleyber Torres, Jurickson Profar, Elvis Andrus

Following prospects can be challenging. First of all, there are just *so many names*. You can't remember Steve from Accounting's name half the time. Wait, is it Tim? Pretty sure it's Tim. Anyways, it's also tough because prospects will break your heart. And let's be honest, there's only so much of your heart available for rent. Can you really give it to a teenager you've never seen before who plays half a continent away? You might want to do just that in the case of Perdomo, an under-the-radar international signing who's started to make significant noise. He's physical in the box, the bat speed is noteworthy and he can make all of the plays at shortstop look way too easy for a guy standing 6-foot-2. He popped up big time in 2018 and will get plenty of buzz moving forward.

YEAR	TEAM	LVL	AGE	PA	DRC+	VORP	BABIP	BRR	FRAA	WARP
2017	DDI	RK	17	278	136	20.0	.282	1.4	SS(63): 11.9	3.1
2018	DIA	RK	18	101	173	14.9	.382	2.6	SS(14): 2.6, 2B(8): 0.5	1.3
2018	MSO	RK	18	29	248	6.6	.556	0.4	SS(5): 0.3, 2B(1): -0.2	0.5
2018	YAK	A-	18	127	148	16.1	.359	1.4	SS(30): 3.9	1.3
2019	ARI	MLB	19	251	21	-22.1	.167	-7.6	SS 5, 2B 0	-1.9

Kristian Robinson CF

Born: 12/11/00 Age: 18 Bats: R Throws: R
Height: 6'3" Weight: 190 Origin: International Free Agent, 2017

YEAR	TEAM	LVL	AGE	PA	R	2B	3B	HR	RBI	BB	K	SB	CS	AVG/OBP/SLG
2018	DIA	RK	17	182	35	11	0	4	31	16	46	7	5	.272/.341/.414
2018	MSO	RK	17	74	13	1	0	3	10	11	21	5	3	.300/.419/.467
2019	ARI	MLB	18	251	18	7	0	5	22	5	94	2	1	.156/.172/.253

Comparables: Adalberto Mondesi, Wilmer Flores, Tommy Brown

Kids these days. When they're not flossing or playing with their fidget spinners, they're apparently growing into large, explosive human beings. Robinson is built like a hybrid linebacker and flies like a wide receiver. His stateside debut didn't disappoint, though his youth showed at times, too. He didn't strike out at an extreme clip in either of the rookie leagues he graced, but did show some swing and miss. He also showed patience, walking at a strong clip while sprinkling in seven home runs over his first 57 professional games. More power will undoubtedly come as Robinson continues to learn how to control his at-bats. The biggest international signing for the franchise in recent history looks the part of a player to build around.

YEAR	TEAM	LVL	AGE	PA	DRC+	VORP	BABIP	BRR	FRAA	WARP
2018	DIA	RK	17	182	128	9.5	.351	1.3	CF(26): -5.3, LF(6): -0.9	0.1
2018	MSO	RK	17	74	119	5.9	.405	0.5	CF(10): -2.3, LF(7): 0.4	0.0
2019	ARI	MLB	18	251	8	-19.3	.220	-0.2	CF -1, LF 0	-2.2

Pavin Smith 1B

Born: 02/06/96 Age: 23 Bats: L Throws: L
Height: 6'2" Weight: 210 Origin: Round 1, 2017 Draft (#7 overall)

YEAR	TEAM	LVL	AGE	PA	R	2B	3B	HR	RBI	BB	K	SB	CS	AVG/OBP/SLG
2017	YAK	A-	21	223	34	15	2	0	27	27	24	2	1	.318/.401/.415
2018	VIS	A+	22	504	63	25	1	11	54	57	65	3	2	.255/.343/.392
2019	*ARI*	*MLB*	*23*	*251*	*21*	*9*	*0*	*6*	*26*	*18*	*49*	*0*	*0*	*.195/.252/.315*

Breakout: 9% Improve: 15% Collapse: 0% Attrition: 6% MLB: 15%
Comparables: Alex Romero, David Cooper, Jake Smolinski

Smith's selection seventh overall came as a bit of a surprise. Sure, he profiled as one of the best pure hitters in the 2017 draft, but being limited entirely to first base puts a monumental amount of pressure on the bat. While the University of Virginia is notable for producing hitters with flat swings, Smith has developed some leverage in his. The problem is that it isn't producing. Scouts remain concerned about a lack of bat speed despite the leverage, and his overall power output has failed to live up to expectations. Smith continues to make plenty of contact, but a trade-off for more power would seem a worthy exchange. Without more pop and a revised plan of attack, he's in danger of losing whatever stock he has.

YEAR	TEAM	LVL	AGE	PA	DRC+	VORP	BABIP	BRR	FRAA	WARP
2017	YAK	A-	21	223	166	15.3	.363	-1.8	1B(42): 1.0	0.7
2018	VIS	A+	22	504	112	9.5	.275	-1.1	1B(109): 9.0, RF(1): -0.1	0.6
2019	*ARI*	*MLB*	*23*	*251*	*51*	*-10.8*	*.216*	*-0.6*	*1B 2*	*-0.9*

Yasmany Tomas LF

Born: 11/14/90 Age: 28 Bats: R Throws: R
Height: 6'2" Weight: 250 Origin: International Free Agent, 2014

YEAR	TEAM	LVL	AGE	PA	R	2B	3B	HR	RBI	BB	K	SB	CS	AVG/OBP/SLG
2016	ARI	MLB	25	563	72	30	1	31	83	31	136	2	4	.272/.313/.508
2017	ARI	MLB	26	180	19	11	1	8	32	13	50	0	0	.241/.294/.464
2018	RNO	AAA	27	371	42	22	4	14	65	11	101	2	0	.262/.280/.465
2019	ARI	MLB	28	251	26	12	1	9	32	14	68	1	1	.236/.284/.413

Breakout: 6% Improve: 46% Collapse: 18% Attrition: 19% MLB: 93%
Comparables: Chris Heisey, Xavier Nady, Glenallen Hill

Reno, Nevada is the biggest little city in America. Looking at their municipal brochure, it's easy to see why: there are ample opportunities to enjoy winter sports, fish Pyramid Lake and make $10 million playing for the Triple-A Reno Aces. There is no footage of Tomas on a snowboard or with a fly rod in his hands, but he did rake in the cash while notably *not* raking in the PCL. Demoted from the major-league roster, his line of trade suitors unsurprisingly did not materialize. His signing has been an unmitigated disaster considering the amount of payroll he assumes and the production he's never produced. But at least he can enjoy his time in the biggest little city in America, a setting that makes all of the sense in the world.

YEAR	TEAM	LVL	AGE	PA	DRC+	VORP	BABIP	BRR	FRAA	WARP
2016	ARI	MLB	25	563	106	19.5	.310	-0.8	RF(91): -10.9, LF(60): -8.8	-0.5
2017	ARI	MLB	26	180	82	5.9	.294	-0.3	LF(42): -7.1	-0.7
2018	RNO	AAA	27	371	70	-3.3	.322	-3.4	LF(44): -5.9, 1B(9): -0.3	-1.9
2019	ARI	MLB	28	251	85	1.9	.293	0.0	LF -5, 1B 0	-0.4

Ildemaro Vargas INF
Born: 07/16/91   Age: 27   Bats: B   Throws: R
Height: 6'0"   Weight: 170   Origin: International Free Agent, 2008

YEAR	TEAM	LVL	AGE	PA	R	2B	3B	HR	RBI	BB	K	SB	CS	AVG/OBP/SLG
2016	MOB	AA	24	351	41	15	2	4	19	24	24	8	0	.276/.325/.372
2016	RNO	AAA	24	224	35	13	0	2	18	20	13	13	1	.354/.418/.449
2017	RNO	AAA	25	535	87	35	4	10	65	30	40	8	3	.312/.355/.462
2017	ARI	MLB	25	13	4	1	0	0	4	0	3	0	0	.308/.308/.385
2018	RNO	AAA	26	572	78	31	10	7	54	30	46	10	4	.311/.348/.445
2018	ARI	MLB	26	20	2	0	0	1	4	1	4	1	0	.211/.250/.368
2019	ARI	MLB	27	200	23	9	2	4	19	9	24	3	1	.262/.302/.396

Breakout: 7%   Improve: 25%   Collapse: 4%   Attrition: 18%   MLB: 39%
Comparables: Alex Mejia, Danny Sandoval, Christian Colon

As a society, we don't give Daniel Bernoulli enough credit. Sure, it's easy to overlook 18th century mathematicians, but we really shouldn't. Bernoulli is credited with a bunch of important stuff, like aerodynamics and the conservation of energy. He's also the creator of the economic term "utility." And in that very specific way, he's uniquely linked to Vargas — a guy with no carrying tool besides his utility. He — Vargas not Bernoulli — can play just about anywhere in the infield and basically never strikes out. He's your prototypical 27-year-old utility man who's still looking for a spot on the bench. Even if it's a working man's dream, Vargas' dream is a dream nonetheless.

YEAR	TEAM	LVL	AGE	PA	DRC+	VORP	BABIP	BRR	FRAA	WARP
2016	MOB	AA	24	351	102	12.9	.287	-0.7	SS(77): 7.5, 2B(4): -0.1	1.6
2016	RNO	AAA	24	224	142	19.9	.372	1.3	2B(45): 4.0, SS(6): 1.5	2.0
2017	RNO	AAA	25	535	109	33.4	.319	1.3	2B(93): 11.8, CF(8): -1.8	2.6
2017	ARI	MLB	25	13	85	-0.2	.400	0.1	2B(3): 0.0, 3B(2): -0.1	0.0
2018	RNO	AAA	26	572	99	19.8	.329	-3.8	SS(107): -6.0, 2B(17): -0.1	0.7
2018	ARI	MLB	26	20	93	0.5	.214	0.0	3B(3): 0.3, 2B(2): 0.1	0.1
2019	ARI	MLB	27	200	83	2.5	.279	0.2	3B 1, 2B 1	0.4

Arizona Diamondbacks 2019

Daulton Varsho   C
Born: 07/02/96   Age: 22   Bats: L   Throws: R
Height: 5'10"   Weight: 190   Origin: Round 2, 2017 Draft (#68 overall)

YEAR	TEAM	LVL	AGE	PA	R	2B	3B	HR	RBI	BB	K	SB	CS	AVG/OBP/SLG
2017	YAK	A-	20	212	36	16	3	7	39	17	30	7	2	.311/.368/.534
2018	VIS	A+	21	342	44	11	3	11	44	30	71	19	3	.286/.363/.451
2019	ARI	MLB	22	251	27	9	1	9	30	12	64	5	1	.214/.252/.374

Breakout: 12%   Improve: 40%   Collapse: 0%   Attrition: 34%   MLB: 47%
Comparables: Hank Conger, Francisco Mejia, Chance Sisco

Black holes are pretty neat, just not when they're on your roster. They have the ability to distort the time and space of entities in their proximity, which sounds cool. Diamondbacks catchers over the last five years have seemed to have a similar quality. Buying low on Welington Castillo and, to a lesser extent, Chris Iannetta were shrewd opportunities, but they were never stars. Tuffy Gosewisch, Chris Herrmann, Jeff Mathis and Alex Avila have been, in a vacuum, devoid of any real impact. Meanwhile, Varsho has risen meteorically through the prospect rankings for good reason and he serves as the greatest opportunity for the organization to find a center to their solar system behind the plate. The VarShow isn't far off, as his athleticism has served as a platform for his improved receiving while he still shows plenty in the box to warrant near-top billing.

YEAR	TEAM	LVL	AGE	PA	DRC+	VORP	BABIP	BRR	FRAA	WARP
2017	YAK	A-	20	212	161	24.1	.338	2.4	C(36): 0.8	1.5
2018	VIS	A+	21	342	132	30.4	.341	2.5	C(55): 1.4	1.8
2019	ARI	MLB	22	251	67	1.2	.249	0.5	C 0	0.2

Andy Yerzy C

Born: 07/05/98 Age: 20 Bats: L Throws: R
Height: 6'3" Weight: 215 Origin: Round 2, 2016 Draft (#52 overall)

YEAR	TEAM	LVL	AGE	PA	R	2B	3B	HR	RBI	BB	K	SB	CS	AVG/OBP/SLG
2016	DIA	RK	17	110	5	3	0	1	15	4	22	0	0	.196/.220/.255
2016	MSO	RK	17	62	2	2	0	0	1	0	16	0	1	.250/.274/.283
2017	MSO	RK	18	249	36	12	0	13	45	24	45	0	0	.298/.365/.524
2018	YAK	A-	19	276	30	11	1	8	34	28	67	0	0	.297/.382/.452
2019	ARI	MLB	20	251	19	5	0	9	27	7	80	0	0	.153/.174/.283

Breakout: 3%   Improve: 3%   Collapse: 0%   Attrition: 1%   MLB: 3%
Comparables: Francisco Pena, Carson Kelly, Alex Liddi

Will he catch? Will he, uh, not catch? Those are the most pertinent questions when it comes to Yerzy. The answers haven't been entirely decided, but one would lean toward the latter. Yerzy has found some consistency and pounds the ball frequently while getting on base. He's not the quickest, most flexible or most fluid receiver, though. The arm plays and he's worked hard to improve, with some of that work paying off. And therein lies the third question: how much can a 20-year-old still improve his catching? Yerzy's bat would project as above average for a catcher, but trends below average if he has to play first base. It's an interesting experiment and the D-backs are unlikely to give up on the idea of him catching just yet.

YEAR	TEAM	LVL	AGE	PA	DRC+	VORP	BABIP	BRR	FRAA	WARP
2016	DIA	RK	17	110	26	-6.0	.232	-1.2	C(18): -0.3	-0.8
2016	MSO	RK	17	62	33	0.1	.341	0.0	C(15): -0.5	-0.3
2017	MSO	RK	18	249	118	15.3	.323	-2.6	C(37): -0.4	0.6
2018	YAK	A-	19	276	139	17.1	.380	-4.4	C(44): -1.0, 1B(8): -0.8	0.5
2019	ARI	MLB	20	251	17	-15.8	.180	-0.6	C -1, 1B 0	-1.8

Taylor Clarke RHP

Born: 05/13/93 Age: 26 Bats: R Throws: R
Height: 6'4" Weight: 200 Origin: Round 3, 2015 Draft (#76 overall)

YEAR	TEAM	LVL	AGE	W	L	SV	G	GS	IP	H	HR	BB/9	K/9	K	GB%	BABIP
2016	KNC	A	23	3	2	0	6	6	28²	24	1	1.6	7.5	24	32%	.277
2016	VIS	A+	23	1	1	0	4	4	23	19	3	2.7	8.6	22	31%	.262
2016	MOB	AA	23	8	6	0	17	17	97²	99	9	1.9	6.6	72	38%	.297
2017	WTN	AA	24	9	7	0	21	21	111¹	94	7	3.2	8.6	107	40%	.292
2017	RNO	AAA	24	3	2	0	6	6	33²	29	8	3.5	8.3	31	34%	.231
2018	RNO	AAA	25	13	8	0	27	27	152	149	12	2.6	7.4	125	40%	.302
2019	ARI	MLB	26	1	1	0	3	3	17	17	3	2.9	8.0	15	38%	.292

Breakout: 7% Improve: 16% Collapse: 8% Attrition: 18% MLB: 40%
Comparables: Kendry Flores, Chris Stratton, D.J. Mitchell

It's Christmas morning and you're bursting at the seams with excitement. At 10 years old, you live for Christmas. It's the pinnacle of being a kid. You get a bunch of stuff you want and literally don't have to do anything to earn it besides show up. French toast breakfast? Check. RC car? Check. Diamondbacks shirsey? Check. The hits just keep coming, then you get the present left by grandma and it's ... a sweater? You've got five of these already and they're all scratchy as hell. Are they useful? Sure, they can be serviceable and there's an application when they're what you need, but like back-end starting pitchers, this sweater isn't getting you excited. You'll keep it and give it a try someday because you basically have to. Can't hurt to have an extra sweater around, even if it's your least exciting Christmas gift.

YEAR	TEAM	LVL	AGE	WHIP	ERA	DRA	WARP	MPH	FB%	WHF	CSP
2016	KNC	A	23	1.01	2.83	3.50	0.5				
2016	VIS	A+	23	1.13	2.74	4.36	0.3				
2016	MOB	AA	23	1.23	3.59	3.26	2.1				
2017	WTN	AA	24	1.19	2.91	4.52	0.9				
2017	RNO	AAA	24	1.25	4.81	4.67	0.4				
2018	RNO	AAA	25	1.27	4.03	4.24	2.2				
2019	ARI	MLB	26	1.26	4.43	4.87	0.0				

Jon Duplantier RHP

Born: 07/11/94 Age: 24 Bats: L Throws: R
Height: 6'4" Weight: 225 Origin: Round 3, 2016 Draft (#89 overall)

YEAR	TEAM	LVL	AGE	W	L	SV	G	GS	IP	H	HR	BB/9	K/9	K	GB%	BABIP
2017	KNC	A	22	6	1	0	13	12	72^2	45	4	1.9	9.7	78	52%	.240
2017	VIS	A+	22	6	2	0	12	12	63^1	46	2	3.8	12.4	87	53%	.324
2018	WTN	AA	23	5	1	0	14	14	67	52	4	3.8	9.1	68	56%	.282
2019	ARI	MLB	24	1	1	0	3	3	15	13	2	4.8	9.4	16	44%	.294

Breakout: 10% Improve: 23% Collapse: 22% Attrition: 42% MLB: 51%
Comparables: Brian Johnson, P.J. Walters, Chris Reed

Duplantier was the Diamondbacks' top prospect a year ago and is still regarded quite highly. But no one would blame you if you aren't totally excited about him. In the plus column, he's nearly big-league ready, has general command of his pitches and has yielded strong results. On the other side of the ledger, he missed time last season with an injury and his numbers weren't great, just good. The injury, of course, is the most worrisome. He pitched a bunch as a Rice Owl and dealt with shoulder issues there. He missed time right after he was drafted with a barking elbow, then suffered from biceps tendinitis in 2018. The latest entry into his injury history is the least concerning, but the whole of it remains a worry. TINSTAAPP is alive and well at the top of Arizona's prospect heap.

YEAR	TEAM	LVL	AGE	WHIP	ERA	DRA	WARP	MPH	FB%	WHF	CSP
2017	KNC	A	22	0.83	1.24	3.41	1.6				
2017	VIS	A+	22	1.15	1.56	2.58	2.0				
2018	WTN	AA	23	1.19	2.69	4.70	0.5				
2019	ARI	MLB	24	1.38	4.17	4.58	0.1				

Merrill Kelly RHP

Born: 10/14/88   Age: 30   Bats: R   Throws: R
Height: 6'2"   Weight: 190   Origin: Round 8, 2010 Draft (#251 overall)

YEAR	TEAM	LVL	AGE	W	L	SV	G	GS	IP	H	HR	BB/9	K/9	K	GB%	BABIP
2019	ARI	MLB	30	8	8	0	23	23	131	125	16	3.3	8.3	121	48%	.293

Breakout: 7%   Improve: 38%   Collapse: 31%   Attrition: 9%   MLB: 94%
Comparables: Doug Davis, Yovani Gallardo, Travis Wood

Tampa Bay's eighth-round pick in 2010, Kelly pitched reasonably well in the minors and advanced to Triple-A in 2014, but never received a call-up. He headed to Korea at age 26, putting together a three-season run as one of the top starting pitchers in the extremely hitter-friendly KBO. He topped 180 innings in all three seasons, posting a combined 3.80 ERA compared to a league average of 5.02. Now he'll hope to follow the path most recently taken by Miles Mikolas, returning to MLB after success in a foreign league turned more heads than previous work in the American minors. Kelly inked a two-year, $5.5 million deal with the Diamondbacks that includes cheap team options for 2021 and 2022. Expecting him to "replace" Patrick Corbin is beyond wishful thinking — Kelly was never considered a top prospect in America and there's nothing dominant about his numbers in Korea — but he has a chance to be a useful back-of-the-rotation starter for Arizona.

YEAR	TEAM	LVL	AGE	WHIP	ERA	DRA	WARP	MPH	FB%	WHF	CSP
2019	ARI	MLB	30	1.30	4.13	4.54	0.8				

Yoan Lopez   RHP

Born: 01/02/93   Age: 26   Bats: R   Throws: R
Height: 6'3"   Weight: 185   Origin: International Free Agent, 2015

YEAR	TEAM	LVL	AGE	W	L	SV	G	GS	IP	H	HR	BB/9	K/9	K	GB%	BABIP
2016	MOB	AA	23	4	7	0	14	14	62	67	10	4.6	5.2	36	42%	.285
2017	VIS	A+	24	2	0	4	20	0	30^2	16	2	2.6	16.4	56	49%	.298
2018	WTN	AA	25	2	6	12	45	0	61^2	38	4	3.8	12.7	87	37%	.258
2018	ARI	MLB	25	0	0	0	10	0	9	7	2	1.0	11.0	11	56%	.238
2019	ARI	MLB	26	2	2	0	40	0	42	34	5	4.6	11.1	53	40%	.291

Breakout: 12%   Improve: 25%   Collapse: 8%   Attrition: 19%   MLB: 35%
Comparables: Daniel Stumpf, Barrett Astin, Ryan Brasier

Lopez signed with the Diamondbacks for a record $8.25 million out of Cuba in 2015, threatened to quit baseball in 2016 due to what the team called "serious emotional issues" and has since shifted to the bullpen full time while developing into a solid prospect. Called up for the first time in September, his big-time fastball velocity took him straight from Double-A to the majors. Lopez doesn't project as a relief ace and he'll likely begin 2019 back in the minors, but in time he should get a chance to claim a setup role.

YEAR	TEAM	LVL	AGE	WHIP	ERA	DRA	WARP	MPH	FB%	WHF	CSP
2016	MOB	AA	23	1.60	5.52	4.18	0.7				
2017	VIS	A+	24	0.82	0.88	1.86	1.1				
2018	WTN	AA	25	1.04	2.92	2.78	1.6				
2018	ARI	MLB	25	0.89	3.00	3.84	0.1	98.6	67.2	13.3	54.2
2019	ARI	MLB	26	1.30	3.86	4.24	0.3	98.2	68.4	13.5	55.2

Arizona Diamondbacks 2019

Taylor Widener   RHP
Born: 10/24/94   Age: 24   Bats: L   Throws: R
Height: 6'0"   Weight: 195   Origin: Round 12, 2016 Draft (#368 overall)

YEAR	TEAM	LVL	AGE	W	L	SV	G	GS	IP	H	HR	BB/9	K/9	K	GB%	BABIP
2016	STA	A-	21	2	0	1	6	1	15^1	2	0	2.3	14.7	25	57%	.095
2016	CSC	A	21	1	0	3	7	1	23	15	2	1.2	13.3	34	38%	.289
2017	TAM	A+	22	7	8	0	27	27	119^1	87	5	3.8	9.7	129	45%	.273
2018	WTN	AA	23	5	8	0	26	25	137^1	99	12	2.8	11.5	176	37%	.275
2019	ARI	MLB	24	1	1	0	3	3	15	12	2	3.4	10.2	17	38%	.293

Breakout: 16%   Improve: 28%   Collapse: 22%   Attrition: 32%   MLB: 61%
Comparables: Yefrey Ramirez, Jharel Cotton, Jake Arrieta

Widener was a sneaky grab for the Diamondbacks when they shipped Brandon Drury and Anthony Banda away to the Yankees and Rays, respectively. He didn't get a ton of buzz in a deep Yankees system, but immediately drew attention on the Diamondbacks' farm due to the lack of quality prospects around him and his excellent results. He murdered Double-A hitters all year in Jackson and sits firmly among the Diamondbacks' best prospects. What's that all worth? Maybe a lot, maybe a little. Scouts have wondered if a move to the bullpen isn't the best course of action, but his most recent campaign as a starter likely bought him at least another year in a rotation. He's added velocity and the slider can be an out pitch, but the emergence of a serviceable changeup might be what keeps him around as a starter long term.

YEAR	TEAM	LVL	AGE	WHIP	ERA	DRA	WARP	MPH	FB%	WHF	CSP
2016	STA	A-	21	0.39	0.00	2.14	0.5				
2016	CSC	A	21	0.78	0.78	2.00	0.8				
2017	TAM	A+	22	1.15	3.39	3.37	2.6				
2018	WTN	AA	23	1.03	2.75	3.06	3.6				
2019	ARI	MLB	24	1.20	3.78	4.15	0.2				

LINEOUTS

Hitters

HITTER	POS	TEAM	LVL	AGE	PA	R	2B	3B	HR	RBI	BB	K	SB	CS	AVG/OBP/SLG	DRC+	WARP
Blaze Alexander	SS	DIA	Rk	19	118	25	10	2	2	25	19	21	7	3	.362/.475/.574	218	0.9
	SS	MSO	Rk	19	129	27	9	3	3	17	12	31	3	0	.302/.364/.509	113	0.9
Jorge Barrosa	CF	DDI	Rk	17	241	57	8	3	3	21	25	34	37	6	.299/.402/.412	148	3.0
	CF	DIA	Rk	17	47	4	0	2	0	1	3	6	2	2	.233/.298/.326	98	0.2
Socrates Brito	RF	RNO	AAA	25	478	85	34	5	17	69	44	104	15	4	.318/.383/.540	136	3.6
	RF	ARI	MLB	25	44	3	0	0	1	3	3	9	0	1	.175/.227/.250	83	0.0
Kevin Cron	3B	RNO	AAA	25	438	57	28	1	22	97	36	100	1	0	.309/.368/.554	126	2.2
Drew Ellis	3B	VIS	A+	22	502	57	34	1	15	71	52	98	2	6	.246/.331/.429	100	-1.3
Caleb Joseph	C	NOR	AAA	32	97	10	2	0	2	14	8	19	0	0	.273/.340/.364	118	0.4
	C	BAL	MLB	32	280	28	14	2	3	17	10	68	2	1	.219/.254/.321	69	-0.1
Domingo Leyba	2B	WTN	AA	22	358	43	17	2	5	30	35	46	5	2	.269/.344/.381	114	0.5
Rob Refsnyder	RF	TBA	MLB	27	103	10	3	0	2	5	18	26	0	2	.167/.314/.274	86	-0.1
	RF	DUR	AAA	27	208	31	10	0	4	15	18	46	0	0	.283/.357/.402	118	0.3
Matt Szczur	OF	SDN	MLB	28	84	11	3	0	1	6	8	24	3	0	.187/.265/.267	61	-0.2
	OF	ELP	AAA	28	43	4	3	1	0	6	4	7	0	0	.316/.372/.447	103	0.0
Alek Thomas	CF	DIA	Rk	18	138	24	3	5	0	10	13	18	8	2	.325/.394/.431	167	0.4
	CF	MSO	Rk	18	134	26	11	1	2	17	11	19	4	3	.341/.396/.496	160	0.8
Kelby Tomlinson	MI	SAC	AAA	28	204	15	2	0	0	10	18	44	7	4	.304/.365/.315	91	0.2
	MI	SFN	MLB	28	152	9	4	2	0	10	9	35	0	2	.207/.265/.264	56	-0.5
Christian Walker	1B	RNO	AAA	27	359	68	25	4	18	71	26	86	1	0	.299/.354/.568	117	0.9
	1B	ARI	MLB	27	53	6	2	0	3	6	3	22	1	0	.163/.226/.388	59	-0.1
Marcus Wilson	CF	VIS	A+	21	502	60	26	2	10	48	44	141	16	6	.235/.309/.369	82	0.0

Blaze Alexander's first name avails itself well to puns, but it's also a healthy descriptor for his game. He's got a cannon of an arm and is known for making loud, laser-like contact. An exciting prospect for his merits and his moniker. ⓧ Kristian Robinson got most of the buzz in Arizona's 2017 J2 class, but don't overlook the diminutive **Jorge Barrosa**. He's a lock to stick in center field and has potential as a leadoff hitter with on-base skills, a contact-oriented approach and enough speed to be a threat on the bases. Oh, and he started switch-hitting in 2018. ⓧ **Socrates Brito** isn't a prospect anymore. He was skipped over to fill J.D. Martinez's departure and has a murky future. He's 26 now and has done it all in Triple-A while mostly falling on his face in the majors. Philosophically, he's built for minor-league depth despite some interesting tools. ⓧ **Kevin Cron** continues to put up impressive minor-league numbers and even got some time at third base in Reno. He's also 26, has never taken a big-league at-bat and is blocked at both corners. ⓧ Drafted in 2017 out of a good Louisville program, nearly half of **Drew Ellis**' hits in 2018 were for extra bases. His defense at third base continues to draw skepticism, however. With questions about his ability to make contact as he climbs the ladder, he'll need to ensure that he's a capable defender because a move to first base may just sink his ship. ⓧ Inexplicably, **Caleb Joseph** went from one of baseball's best-rated defensive catchers in 2017 to one of the worst in 2018. With an offensive downturn across the board, it's not hard to see him on the short end of the platoon with Chance Sisco or even losing out the backup job to similar defensive standout Austin Wynns. ⓧ **Domingo Leyba** took to the field again in 2018 after missing most of the previous season with a shoulder injury. There's still potential here for a second-division starter, but anything short of that will turn him into a Quadruple-A player given a lack of defensive versatility. ⓧ Teams keeping picking up **Rob Refsnyder** and giving him a chance in the majors due to hypothetical versatility, but he's neither a good defender nor a good hitter. ⓧ **Matt Szczur** was designated for assignment last summer, the latest casualty in baseball's march to vanquish fifth outfielders from big-league rosters. When he's not busy painting or punning his name on Twitter, he'll probably be giving Triple-A lefties and announcers fits in equal measure. ⓧ **Alek Thomas'** pro debut was encouraging. He proved capable of hitting rookie-level pitching at two stops, notching strong averages while controlling the strike zone and making plenty of contact. His profile is that of a strong defender in center field with bat control, some on-base skills and enough speed to do additional damage. ⓧ Punch-and-Judy hitters like **Kelby Tomlinson** are unfashionable these days, and the bespectacled infielder doesn't play shortstop well enough to compensate for his powerless bat. ⓧ **Christian Walker** destroyed Triple-A pitching. *Again.* The righty-swinger has a ton of power and put it to use in Reno, but that output didn't exactly translate to the majors. *Again.* ⓧ **Marcus Wilson**'s strong 2017 was a bright spot for a down system. A move to the California League in 2018 was supposed to cement his status, but the toolsy center fielder struggled against better pitching. A late-season surge helped salvage some value.

Pitchers

PITCHER	TEAM	LVL	AGE	W	L	SV	G	GS	IP	H	HR	BB/9	K/9	K	GB%	WHIP	ERA	DRA	WARP
Joseph Krehbiel	ARI	MLB	25	0	0	0	2	0	3	1	0	6.0	0.0	0	40%	1.00	0.00	9.38	-0.2
	RNO	AAA	25	3	3	2	48	0	57^1	49	9	3.9	11.1	71	46%	1.29	4.24	3.34	1.2
Artie Lewicki	TOL	AAA	26	5	6	0	12	12	61^2	64	5	2.3	8.0	55	42%	1.30	4.67	3.88	1.2
	DET	MLB	26	0	2	0	13	3	38^2	48	4	3.3	7.0	30	42%	1.60	4.89	5.45	-0.2
Matt Mercer	YAK	A-	21	0	0	0	12	12	27	19	1	2.0	12.3	37	48%	0.93	3.00	1.95	1.0
Jared Miller	RNO	AAA	24	1	3	0	38	0	42	46	6	13.5	11.1	52	47%	2.60	7.71	4.15	0.5
	WTN	AA	24	0	0	0	6	0	6	3	0	6.0	10.5	7	77%	1.17	1.50	2.75	0.2
Marc Rzepczynski	SEA	MLB	32	0	1	0	18	0	7^2	13	2	10.6	11.7	10	61%	2.87	9.39	3.36	0.1
	CLE	MLB	32	0	0	0	5	0	2^2	3	0	3.4	3.4	1	62%	1.50	0.00	5.48	0.0
	TAC	AAA	32	0	0	0	12	0	9^1	15	2	7.7	9.6	10	66%	2.46	9.64	4.18	0.1
Robby Scott	PAW	AAA	28	3	3	3	45	0	48^1	35	1	3.9	11.7	63	43%	1.16	1.86	2.32	1.5
	BOS	MLB	28	0	1	0	9	0	6^2	10	2	6.8	10.8	8	23%	2.25	8.10	8.96	-0.3
Braden Shipley	ARI	MLB	26	0	0	0	3	0	5	4	0	3.6	5.4	3	47%	1.20	7.20	5.26	0.0
	RNO	AAA	26	6	4	1	30	6	74^1	93	13	4.4	7.0	58	38%	1.74	5.81	7.30	-1.7
Matt Tabor	YAK	A-	19	2	1	0	14	14	60^2	59	4	1.9	6.8	46	45%	1.19	3.26	3.92	0.9
Emilio Vargas	VIS	A+	21	8	5	0	20	19	108	92	7	3.4	11.7	140	40%	1.23	2.50	4.03	1.6
	WTN	AA	21	1	3	0	6	6	35^2	31	6	2.0	7.6	30	44%	1.09	4.04	3.77	0.7

Joseph Krehbiel finally got his cup of coffee after a minor-league career full of decent seasons. He can run it up into the upper 90s, but it's a flat-ish fastball and the secondaries lack much depth. He appears destined for up-and-down work. ⓧ Swingman **Artie Lewicki** will miss all of 2019 following his second Tommy John surgery. ⓧ **Tim Locastro** has four vowels in his name, but somehow they're not all "A", which would have been apropos of his status as a decent Quad-A hurler. ⓧ **Matt Mercer**'s pro debut flew under the radar after his fifth-round selection from the state of Oregon's second-best program. Pitching as a starter on a short leash, the delivery has some effort and violence to it. In the Northwest League playoffs he was running the heater up to 98, showing a get-me-over curve and flashing a good changeup. ⓧ **Jared Miller** is a poster boy for the "minor league relievers are hard to predict" movement. He looked like a real Dude for the vast majority of 2016 and 2017, before 2018 rolled around and he basically fell flat on his face. The hulking lefty has a lot to keep in check in the mechanics department and refinement is needed. ⓧ The "other" **Cody Reed** remains an enigma. The former second-round pick has posted up-and-down results without any semblance of stability as the scouting reports haven't matched the occasionally great stats. He missed all of 2018 with injury and the lefty will almost surely be moved to relief. ⓧ In 2018 **Marc Rzepczynski** lost his command, lost his job, lost his spot in Seattle, and for all we know lost his dog too. What he didn't lose was his contract, which paid $5.5 million dollars last year. Admittedly that part doesn't make for a great country song. ⓧ Looking for

Arizona Diamondbacks 2019

one New Englander who didn't love Alex Cora's managerial debut? Try LOOGY **Robby Scott**, who spent almost all year stuck in Pawtucket thanks to a roster crunch and spotty command. ⓘ **Braden Shipley**, a 2013 first-round pick, had a dismal 2018. He transitioned to a relief role and couldn't find any traction. He still fails to strike batters out while giving away too many free passes and round trips. It's hard to see how he fits, or rather *if* he fits at all. ⓘ **Matt Tabor** is an intelligent pitcher with some projection remaining. The projection is important because the stuff, in its current form, isn't exciting. He routinely sat 89-92 with inconsistent secondaries. He was able to generate some easy ground-ball outs, however, and was rarely hit hard. ⓘ **Emilio Vargas** was the California League pitcher of the year and his development as a pitcher, rather than a thrower, paid dividends. He can touch 96 when really humping it and mixes his secondaries (a slider and change) well. A jump to Double-A didn't go as smoothly, but there's hope here for a back-end starter.

Diamondbacks Prospects

The State of the System:
It's not the deepest system in the world, but we are on one straight year of it being an okay system, and man does that feel weird to type.

The Top Ten:

1 **Jazz Chisholm SS**   OFP: 60   Likely: 50   ETA: Early 2020
Born: 02/01/98   Age: 21   Bats: L   Throws: R   Height: 5'11"   Weight: 165
Origin: International Free Agent, 2015

The Report: Look, I already spent an entire blurb this year debating the role of aesthetics in prospect evaluation, so there is no way I am not going to be enamored with a dude who dresses up like Black Panther to hit huge batting practice dingers. Jazz—I'm invoking the Bartolo rule from the style guide here—had me long before that, though. He's a quick-twitch, potential plus-or-better shortstop. That's a pretty big box checked off in the heart of any prospect writer. With plus actions, plus arm, plus range, and uh, plus raw (and that's not power in this case), Jazz is never boring on any ball hit in his vicinity, and he's capable of the spectacular.

At the plate? Well, Jazz is more Pharoah Sanders than John Coltrane at present. He swings hard and generates more power than you'd think out of his wiry frame, although he pays for it with substantial swing and miss. He might have to find a compromise between the natural fluidity of his swing and his aggressive, power-minded approach. But even Coltrane recorded *Om* eventually (though I don't suggest Jazz take the same approach with his pre-game preparations) and if the hit tool doesn't come around, he might not have enough of a career to merit any future critical reevaluation.

The Risks: High. There's still a fair bit of risk in the bat, and Double-A will provide a crucial test for the profile.

Ben Carsley's Fantasy Take: As you can likely tell already, Jazz is a much better IRL than fantasy prospect. That being said, there's enough to like here since we're dealing with a dude who's a lock to stay at short, who can hit for some power, and who might only be a year-and-a-half away. In short, I wouldn't ever expect Chisholm to ever perform as a top-10 shortstop, but he might be able to hit for enough power and steal just enough bases to become a top-20 option. This is not the most exciting fantasy system…

Arizona Diamondbacks 2019

2 **Jon Duplantier RHP**   OFP: 60   Likely: 50   ETA: 2019
Born: 07/11/94   Age: 24   Bats: L   Throws: R   Height: 6'4"   Weight: 225
Origin: Round 3, 2016 Draft (#89 overall)

The Report: The old Good/Bad format would work well for this dude. Duplantier has a lot of good—a full four-pitch mix where each could become average with upside from there. There's a lively low-to-mid-90s fastball that hitters beat into the ground, and the trendy hard slider works well in concert for swings-and-misses. His curve flashes plus too, and he also throws a changeup that might get to average or slightly better. As you'd imagine for an advanced true four-pitch guy, he's run into little trouble so far in the minors through Double-A.

So what's the bad? We've noted in the past that he's a control-over-command guy, but he's started walking people more than we anticipated. There's effort and violence in the delivery, and 2017 is the only season in college or pro ball that he's stayed healthy while starting. You could very easily see him consolidating the repertoire down to feature the fastball and slider, transitioning to a relief role, and never looking back.

The Risks: High. "Starting pitcher from Rice" is its own entire category of red flag. Duplantier missed about two months this summer with biceps tendinitis. He has also had significant elbow trouble earlier in his career, and battled shoulder problems in college. So there's a lot of injury risk here on top of the scouty reliever risk.

Ben Carsley's Fantasy Take: I want to like Duplantier from a dynasty perspective because I think he'll be fun to watch, but I'm comparatively low on him as a fantasy guy. As noted above, there probably isn't elite strikeout potential here, and now it looks less likely to come with a sparkly WHIP to mitigate the lack of Ks. Add in the durability/reliever concerns and you get a guy who I think is fairly overvalued in dynasty. He's a solid prospect to be sure, and one who may still fight his way onto the 101, but I think he's a touch overrated in our world right now.

3 **Kristian Robinson OF**   OFP: 60   Likely: 50   ETA: 2023
Born: 12/11/00   Age: 18   Bats: R   Throws: R   Height: 6'3"   Weight: 190
Origin: International Free Agent, 2017

The Report: Jarrett Seidler waxed about Bahamian prospects in our Angels list, but Robinson is the crown jewel of that talented 2017 class. With a frame (and tools profile) that is essentially a Jo Adell starter kit, we were always going to be smitten with him. There's explosive bat speed and his approach improved throughout his first pro season. He's a good bet to stick in center field even if he fills out in his late teens and twenties. He's potentially plus-or-better in the four tools you really care about (the arm is light). Robinson offers the kind of upside you dream about in an outfield prospect; you don't have to squint hard to see a 20/20 center fielder.

He's also another prospect who fits well in our old Good/Bad format. There's significant swing-and-miss. He can get a little out of control at the plate. He's still likely four or more years away from paydirt. Conversely, he's still a prospect who doesn't fit all that well into our OFP/Likely format because of the rigidness of our application. I also don't get to punt it for another year. Let's just say the positive and negative risk here stretches well beyond what's below and reconvene this time next year—where it's entirely possible I will be making the same apologies I made for being a year late on (insert complex league breakout prospect of choice). Unlike Vladito, I will at least make sure he's *on* the 101 this time.

The Risks: High. He spent all of 2018 in short-season ball as a 17-year-old. As good as the tools are here, the delta is gonna be high.

Ben Carsley's Fantasy Take: The odds may be long, but anytime you get an athlete with Robinson's power/speed combination you have to pay attention as a fantasy owner. Robinson already had some buzz last year, so he may be owned already in more serious leagues. But if you're looking for an all-upside flier or your leaguemates haven't caught on yet he's a fine addition in formats with 150-plus prospects rostered.

4. Daulton Varsho   C
OFP: 60   Likely: 50   ETA: Late 2020
Born: 07/02/96   Age: 22   Bats: L   Throws: R   Height: 5'10"   Weight: 190
Origin: Round 2, 2017 Draft (#68 overall)

The Report: In addition to sounding like a protagonist from a *Walking Tall* direct-to-video sequel, Varsho carries the requisite big stick. Despite his cold-weather catching pedigree, he handled the Cal League with little issue and projects for above-average power with enough facility with the bat to get most of it into games. The biggest question with Varsho was a familiar one to anyone who spends too much (any) time thinking about catching prospects: Will he stick? The frame is more Joe Don Baker than The Rock, which is the only instance that isn't a demerit, and he has an easy plus arm. His receiving has improved throughout his pro career, although it still remains fringy for now. The upper minors will give us a better idea if Varsho is an A-List catching prospect or just another Kevin Sorbo. For now, the audition tape is promising.

The Risks: High. Catchers are weird. Cold weather catchers with glove questions are just risky.

Ben Carsley's Fantasy Take: Varsho would be a good dynasty catching prospect if they existed, but, as we've chronicled many, many times, they really don't. Hopefully Varsho still has catching eligibility a few seasons into his career when he's ready to hit MLB pitching. If so, he could easily be a top-7 catcher. He could also be a Quad-A first baseman at that point, a la Peter O'Brien. He should be owned in TDGX-sized leagues with 200-plus prospects rostered, but he shouldn't be on our dynasty top-101.

Arizona Diamondbacks 2019

5 **Taylor Widener   RHP**   OFP: 55   Likely: 50   ETA: 2019
Born: 10/24/94   Age: 24   Bats: L   Throws: R   Height: 6'0"   Weight: 195
Origin: Round 12, 2016 Draft (#368 overall)

The Report: This was my 2018 sleeper prospect coming out of the EL playoffs, so you can't say we didn't try to give you a heads up. Suffice to say, the sleeper woke up big after a spring trade to Arizona, decimating the Southern League and working his way into the 101 conversation. As we've noted often in the past, the Yankees grow major-college sleeper pitchers on trees—they found Widener as a 12th-round college swingman out of South Carolina.

Widener works consistently in the low-to-mid-90s with the fastball. He commands and manipulates the pitch extremely well, which is the basis for most successful starting pitching prospects. He also has a potential plus slider, although it gets a little slurvy occasionally, and a change that flashes average. The command of his secondary offerings lags behind the fastball at present, although he's getting better here. He could end up in the rotation or the bullpen longer term.

The Risks: Medium. He's a converted reliever, but he's stayed healthy and pitched well in the rotation for two years now. He's on the smaller side and will need more consistency with his secondaries to start in the big leagues. He's a bit of a matched pair with Duplantier.

Ben Carsley's Fantasy Take: Well, on the one hand it's fair to call Widener underrated from a dynasty POV, because I feel like lots of people have barely heard of him. On the other hand, there isn't a ton of upside to get excited about here. So in deep leagues with 200-plus guys owned? Sure, Widener makes a nice pickup. In shallower formats? You can probably wait until he's in the majors to make him a streaming option.

6 **Alek Thomas   OF**   OFP: 55   Likely: 45   ETA: 2022
Born: 04/28/00   Age: 19   Bats: L   Throws: L   Height: 5'11"   Weight: 175
Origin: Round 2, 2018 Draft (#63 overall)

The Report: Despite not signing their first-round pick, Arizona came away from the 2018 draft far from empty-handed. Thomas was a football and baseball commit to TCU and you can see it in his sturdy, athletic frame. Despite being a multisport star in high school, his baseball skills are quite advanced for his age and profile. He's also a bit of a bloodlines prospect, as his father Allen is the strength and conditioning director for the White Sox and played a couple seasons in the minors himself. The junior Thomas is a quick-twitch up the middle type with a loose and pretty left-handed swing. He has good wrists and plus bat speed, as well as some innate feel for hitting. It's a line-drive oriented swing that's not going to project for much game power, so Thomas fits best as a top-of-the-order, slash-and-dash type center fielder. He makes a useful matched set with Jake McCarthy; Thomas offers more in the way of upside, but also a bit more variance and risk. Like I always say, it's good to diversify your center fielders.

The Risks: High. There is a limited pro track record. Power projection might limit the ceiling.

Ben Carsley's Fantasy Take: Thomas is a solid watch-list guy as a toolsy project who's too raw and far away to get truly excited about right now, but who could shoot up lists if the bat looks good against more legit competition.

7 Jake McCarthy   OF   OFP: 55   Likely: 45   ETA: 2021
Born: 07/30/97   Age: 21   Bats: L   Throws: L   Height: 6'3"   Weight: 195
Origin: Round 1, 2018 Draft (#39 overall)

The Report: McCarthy is another in the recurring series of "good center field gloves with a chance to hit" that we have all come to know and love (well, maybe less love from Ben). The comp-round pick plays aggressively in center field, with good instincts on the grass and the closing speed to go get it in the gaps. The glove is going to be the carrying tool here but it is potentially plus.

McCarthy isn't a zero at the plate either. Like many UVA hitters, his approach and swing is geared toward hitting line drives up the middle. He lacks the leg drive or lift to project for much pop, but may add enough strength to run into a few pull side. The more likely scenario is that he sprays the gaps and uses his plus speed to take a few extra bases. The other scenario we have to consider is that better velocity, sequencing, and positioning erode enough of his hit tool to make him more of a useful fourth outfielder than a regular.

The Risks: Medium. The defensive skills make for a nice base but he has run himself into some injuries with his style of play. While I don't expect a college performer like McCarthy to struggle in full-season ball, he hasn't hit there yet.

Ben Carsley's Fantasy Take: Less love from Ben is right. McCarthy's only path to fantasy value is to become an accumulator, which means we shouldn't have interest in him until and unless it looks like he'll be playing often. His glove is good enough that such a future is possible, but if it does come to fruition it won't be terribly exciting.

8 Blaze Alexander   SS   OFP: 55   Likely: 45   ETA: 2022
Born: 06/11/99   Age: 20   Bats: R   Throws: R   Height: 6'0"   Weight: 160
Origin: Round 11, 2018 Draft (#339 overall)

The Report: I suppose with his above-average speed you can chalk one up to nominative determinism here, but really the more appropriate appellation would be "Canon" Alexander. I guess if we really want to stretch things, we could suggest that the blaze refers to the smoke trail left behind by his throws. But however you hamfistedly describe it, Alexander has a gun for an arm. It's a plus-plus rocket launcher (there, that was easy enough in the end). The rest of the tools play well at the six too. He's a plus athlete with good hands and actions. The arm is just as sturdy on the move as it is planted deep in the hole, and his lean frame could add plenty of good weight while sticking at shortstop. The question with Alexander coming into June was the bat. While you'd think his post-draft performance would assuage those concerns, he did most of his damage in the Pioneer League, which offers about as much gravitational pull on baseballs as the surface of the moon. This is a bit of an oversimplification of the results/run environment, but Alexander's .873 OPS for Missoula was only good for a 101 DRC+. We don't scout the (advanced) statline here, but I do worry that Alexander lacks a bit of physicality at the plate and can overswing and lose barrel control. There's pretty good bat speed though, and I wouldn't be surprised if he develops sneaky pop either. This 2018 draft troika represents a neat little tier for me and I'd be amenable to any order depending on what you want to emphasize. Alexander would definitely top the tier on name value (though not the system—Jazz Chisholm is the easiest 80-grade I'll give out all winter).

The Risks: High. Like most IMG guys, Alexander is a little bit older for a prep bat, if that matters to you. He also has a limited pro track record and there are questions about the ultimate projection with the bat.

Ben Carsley's Fantasy Take: Ah, so he is… a worse offensive version of Jazz Chisholm. Tempting, but watch list at best for now.

9 Pavin Smith 1B

OFP: 50   Likely: 45   ETA: 2020
Born: 02/06/96   Age: 23   Bats: L   Throws: L   Height: 6'2"   Weight: 210
Origin: Round 1, 2017 Draft (#7 overall)

The Report: This may be a bit harsh on Smith, who did about what you'd expect given the pre-2018 report when he ranked second in the system. Arizona's farm is much better though, while Smith's range of outcomes has seemingly narrowed after he slugged .392 in the California League. The good remains the same. Smith has great bat control and can cover just about any part of the zone. He also understands the strike zone well and passes on offerings that would send most others fishing. He's a natural hitter. He's also a first baseman and, aye, there's the rub.

There's some natural inside-out to Smith's swing and not much loft. It's only average bat speed, despite his feel for hitting. He's got a lean frame, but lacks the innate athleticism of the similarly-profiled Evan White. And ultimately, he posted a sub-.400 slugging in the Cal as a college first baseman. So yes, it might be a bit harsh, but there is cause for concern here.

The Risks: Low. I don't think anyone doubts that Smith can hit for average and get on base at a decent clip. The concern is that it won't be a high enough average or OBP for a first baseman with limited pop.

Ben Carsley's Fantasy Take: Yeah you can skip out on this "I'll have the Matt Thaiss special, but milder"-ass first baseman.

10. Domingo Leyba 2B
OFP: 50 Likely: 45 ETA: Late 2019
Born: 09/11/95 Age: 23 Bats: B Throws: R Height: 5'11" Weight: 160
Origin: International Free Agent, 2006

The Report: Leyba bounced back well from his 2017 season-ending shoulder surgery and resumed being extremely Domingo Leyba. I shouldn't like this profile as much as I do, and you can feel free to prefer the toolsier dudes in the next five (or the major-league-ready relievers, if that floats your boat). He's a hit-tool driven second baseman without much in the way of big tools. He's always been more solid than spectacular. His bat control is excellent, but can also lead to suboptimal contact, since he isn't a big power guy; he might scrape double-digit home runs on occasion.

Leyba's a reliable hand at second who could stand at short once a week for you in a pinch. It's a thoroughly uninteresting profile, but for some reason I like it. He's a switch-hitter with good bat control on both sides. He'll work some walks just by virtue of being pesky and fouling off pitches. Leyba may not ever start for a good team, but he's a useful player and he's about ready for the majors.

The Risks: Low. Leyba is healthy, hitting, and unlikely to change much for good or for ill before he is ineligible for a prospect list.

Ben Carsley's Fantasy Take: You don't really need me on this one. You know what (not) to do.

The Next Five:

11. Geraldo Perdomo SS
Born: 10/22/99 Age: 19 Bats: B Throws: R Height: 6'2" Weight: 184
Origin: International Free Agent, 2016

Perdomo isn't that far off the toolsy 19-year-old up-the-middle draftees in the top 10, but his rawness bleeds through a bit more. He's tall and lean, bordering on thin, but projects for average raw power if and when he fills out. He's not quite as fast-twitch as Alexander—and the arm's about two grades lighter—but he's a solid middle infielder with clean actions and footwork. The defensive profile may play better at the keystone than at shortstop, which is why he's just off the main list for now, but his upside with the bat makes his overall upside similar to Thomas and Alexander.

12. Yoan Lopez RHP
Born: 01/02/93 Age: 26 Bats: R Throws: R Height: 6'3" Weight: 185
Origin: International Free Agent, 2015

Lopez has been dominant since a move to the pen in 2017. A 98-and-a-slider guy, the fastball has explosive life up in the zone and it pairs well with a power slider around 85 with good late tilt, although it can get a little slurvy and flat at times. The righty even has a slightly better change than you'd expect—although it can be quite firm, it has a 10+ mph gap that he sells well. The control isn't always ideal, but Lopez moves the ball around the zone well enough given that he's throwing 98 with a plus slider. He's probably not going to throw quite enough strikes to make you feel entirely comfortable with him in the highest leverage roles, but he's a major-league-ready setup option nonetheless.

13 Marcus Wilson   OF
Born: 08/15/96   Age: 22   Bats: R   Throws: R   Height: 6'3"   Weight: 175
Origin: Round 2, 2014 Draft (#69 overall)

I really figured I'd be penciling Wilson somewhere on our 101 this year. While he's not markedly different from the cavalcade of speed-and-glove center fielders you've already read about multiple times on the list and many others, sometimes you just get a feeling. Instead, Wilson struggled mightily in the Cal League in 2018 as he tried tapping into more power and instead merely upped his strikeouts. There are still center-field tools here. He's an above-average runner with good instincts and an average arm. He should add more strength and maybe some fringy pop develops on its own. And he'll only be 22 next season, even if he will likely be repeating Visalia. I'm not giving up yet, even if Wilson needs an overhaul, or at least a reset in the batter's box. Your dudes are your dudes.

14 Jimmie Sherfy   RHP
Born: 12/27/91   Age: 27   Bats: R   Throws: R   Height: 6'0"   Weight: 175
Origin: Round 10, 2013 Draft (#300 overall)

What does Sherfy have to do to get an extended shot in a major league pen? He turned 27 at the end of the year and has dominated the PCL the last two seasons in one of its more unfriendly pitching climes. His fastball is down a tick nowadays, but it's still a lively offering. Sherfy adjusted by leaning heavily on his curveball which is a potential plus offering. That's usually a winning formula for major league relievers nowadays, and it's unclear why Sherfy has toiled away in Reno for so long. He's a bit of a personal cheeseball of mine, but he's also basically a major-league-ready setup guy. That's not without value, even if it doesn't usually set the prospect writer's heart a flutter.

15 Taylor Clarke   RHP
Born: 05/13/93   Age: 26   Bats: R   Throws: R   Height: 6'4"   Weight: 200
Origin: Round 3, 2015 Draft (#76 overall)

Like Pavin Smith, Clarke is a victim of a vastly improved system, because he was very much Taylor Clarke once again in 2018. Working in the low-90s from his long, 6-foot-7 frame and high-three-quarters slot, Clarke creates a tough plane on his heater. While it's far from an overpowering pitch, he will cut it at times and work it in and out to keep it off of barrels. Despite his large humanness, Clarke has above-average command and control.

What Clarke doesn't have is an obvious out pitch. He relies primarily on a low-80s slider, which can get a bit loose and lacks ideal depth. He's comfortable commanding it to either side and can spot it for a strike, but he struggles to entice swings and misses with it out of the zone, and gets hit hard when up and out over the plate. He also offers a mid-70s curveball that has inconsistent shape (although the best ones are solid 11-6 breakers) and a changeup which has 10 mph or so of velo separation but not much fade. The stuff is generally fringy, the command a bit better than that. Clarke ultimately profiles as a backend starter or swing type, albeit not the ideal one for Chase Field, humidor or no.

Others of note:

Andy Yerzy, C, Short-Season Hillsboro

Yerzy is more The Rock than Joe Don Baker and that's a more unusual frame to stick behind the plate. There are some other logical points of divergence with Varsho as well, considering Yerzy was a prep catching pick. There will always be more questions about the glove, given the gap between catching high school arms and pro pitchers. Like many prep catchers, Yerzy got drafted as high as he did because of his bat, specifically the raw pop here. It's second deck, plus raw, but the swing has limited it to occasional pull-side power so far as a pro. Behind the plate, his size limits his lateral agility. Both his receiving and footwork on throws are works in progress. He has the ingredients for an everyday catcher, but that baking time is going to be significant, like a soufflé. And also like a soufflé, there are a lot of ways this could fall flat.

Top Talents 25 and Under (born 4/1/93 or later):

1. Ketel Marte
2. Jazz Chisholm
3. Jon Duplantier
4. Luke Weaver
5. Kristian Robinson
6. Carson Kelly
7. Daulton Varsho
8. Taylor Widener

9. Alek Thomas
10. Jake McCarthy

Arizona doesn't have Taijuan Walker or Archie Bradley young (or in Walker's case healthy) enough to kick around anymore on this list, so the spotlight shifts to last year's fifth-ranked youngin', Ketel Marte. It's coming, that big breakout. He's been creeping towards the day steadily over a 400-game career now, with last year's three-win effort his best big-league season to date. A broad base of skills translates into positive value in all three phases of the game, and the team has floated the idea of deploying him in center next season. Wherever he lands on the defensive spectrum, it's likely to remain an up-the-middle assignment of some kind for the foreseeable future, and with a massively team-friendly deal locking him in place through 2024, he's emerged as one of the more valuable assets around.

From there, the team took its first two steps in the long journey into post-Goldschmidtian viability when they acquired Luke Weaver and Carson Kelly for the former franchise cornerstone. After titillating with a curiously-high strikeout rate as a rookie in St. Louis, Weaver's command regressed and the performance plummeted accordingly in his sophomore campaign. The secondaries both got tattooed too often, and there isn't enough fastball there for him to lean on the pitch as much as he does without exquisite command. The raw material is there for mid-rotation value, and he'll certainly have a longer leash to explore that space in Arizona than he would have in St. Louis.

Kelly's bat has yet to flash big-league utility through three start-and-stop tours now, but stop-and-starts aren't particularly conducive to such pursuits. He's got precious little left to prove in Triple-A, as the glove looks as promising as ever and he's posted a 115 DRC+ with a double-digit walk rate across his last two seasons in Memphis. He should be able to hold down a big-league job for a long time thanks to the leather, and if the bat nudges its way into respectability, I'll have undersold him on this list.

With a transitional period looming it should surprise no one if this list is much more flush with on-the-brink talent this time next year.

Part 3: Featured Articles

The Hole in The Shift is Fixing Itself

Russell Carleton

I've been on a bit of a mission against The Shift of late. I'm not out to get The Shift for the usual reasons that people oppose it. The words "the right way to play the game" won't be found on my lips. If a team wants to pursue a strategy that is within the rules and it works, then by all means, they have my blessing (not that they need it). Instead, my concern with The Shift is a worry that it doesn't work, or at least that it has a flaw that needs fixing.

The data show that while The Shift does a decent job of preventing singles on balls in play (what it's supposed to do), it also increases the number of walks that happen in front of it, and the number of additional walks outweighs the number of singles saved. It's a problem because you can't throw a guy out if he gets to walk to first base.

But the "why" was important. It seemed that The Shift was changing the way in which pitchers pitched. We saw that there were fewer fastballs thrown in front of The Shift than we might otherwise expect, and that pitchers tended to stay out of the strike zone a little more. Not by a lot. In fact, it might not even be visible to the naked eye. The percentage of pitches that are out of the zone goes from 51.0 to 53.3 from a standard defense (two right/two left) to a full shift (three on one side). That difference stands up even after we control for the types of hitters that get shifted against. And it's enough to drive up the walk rate to where it cancels out the benefits that teams thought they were getting with The Shift... and then some.

But there was some hope. I found that when individual pitchers stayed closer to the in-zone/out-of-zone mix that they used without The Shift on, they could still get the benefits of The Shift without the walk problems. So, in theory, a team could simply figure out a way to convince its pitchers to not fall prey to the walk trap and The Shift would once again be their friend.

It's reasonable to think that some teams might be more hip to this idea than others. Maybe some figured it out a year before the others. Maybe they were better at getting the message across to their pitchers. Or, maybe no one has figured it out yet.

Warning! Gory Mathematical Details Ahead!

I used data from 2015-2017, made available through MLB's data portal, Baseball Savant. They are kind enough to note when teams are using an infield shift (three fielders on one side of second base), as opposed to a "strategic shift" (someone's playing a bit out of position, but it's not quite that drastic) or a "standard" alignment.

Since we're doing this by team, I can't just look at raw walk rates, because we know that some teams have good pitchers and others have not-so-good pitchers. Some have a mix of both. I used the log-odds ratio method to take into account a batter's general walking proclivities, and a pitcher's as well, and then shoving them into a binary logistic regression. Then, I asked the computer to generate a specific coefficient for each team's pitchers, for when they went into The Shift and how that affected their walk rate.

Using those coefficients, I was able to project what would happen if a league-average pitcher faced a league-average hitter (which we expect would product a league-average walk rate; from 2015-2017, 7.7 percent of plate appearances ended in a walk) and then just switched his hat. Here's the top five and the bottom five:

Top 5 Teams	Projected Shift Walk Rate	Bottom 5 Teams	Projected Shift Walk Rate
Rockies	6.2%	Rangers	11.2%
Pirates	6.7%	Mets	10.4%
Indians	7.2%	Dodgers	10.2%
Astros	7.3%	Cardinals	9.9%
Braves	7.7%	Tigers	9.7%

There are probably people out there right now trying to figure out what the common thread is among the top and bottom teams. I'm sure, because this is Baseball Prospectus, people are already trying to make the case that sabermetric "early adopters" have some sort of edge here. I think that the more interesting piece is that by the time you get to fifth place in The Shift, we're at league average.

As a sanity check, I examined the issue on a pitch-by-pitch level, looking at how often pitchers threw their pitches in the GameDay strike zone, and again using the same basic methodology and getting team-specific coefficients. The names on the list re-arranged themselves, but the idea was the same, and the two lists correlated with an R of .593.

There's a reason that I don't usually do this type of leaderboard post. I don't really know what the Rockies, Pirates, Indians, Astros, and Braves have in common, or what they have that the bottom five don't. I can put a shrug emoji here and say, "Well, it must be something!" but that seems like a cop-out. Instead, I'd like to present another table and suggest that the table above doesn't even really matter anymore.

Year	League Percent Outside K Zone (Full Shift)	League Percent in K Zone (No Shift)	Difference
2015	54.1%	51.1%	3.0%
2016	53.3%	50.9%	2.4%
2017	52.6%	50.9%	1.7%
2018	52.0%	50.7%	1.3%

The hole in The Shift is fixing itself, and it's coming down really fast league wide. In my earlier work on The Shift, I suggested that until teams stopped having such a huge difference between their out-of-zone rate with and without The Shift on, there would just be too many walks for The Shift to make sense. It seems that all 30 of them have been working toward just that. I once estimated that it takes about 10 years for an idea to filter its way through baseball. At this rate, it looks like teams are going to catch up a lot faster than that. And yeah, they're all saber-smart now.

It's likely that whatever magic it was that the Rockies and Pirates had has made its way to Texas and Queens. Or is at least on its way. And if teams are committing to fixing the walk problem, then it's likely that they will continue shifting and shifting a lot.

And eventually it's going to actually make sense for them to do it.

—*Russell Carleton is a former author of Baseball Prospectus and now an analyst for the New York Mets.*

The State of the Quality Start

Rob Mains

One of the seven things you (probably) didn't know about the 2018 season is that quality starts—defined as a start lasting six or more innings with three or fewer earned runs allowed—as a percentage of total starts cratered to an all-time low of 41 percent. I want to look a little more deeply into this, since it's been a while (May of 2016, to be exact) since I've examined quality starts.

The term *quality start* is credited to *Philadelphia Inquirer* sportswriter John Lowe. It's been derided ever since he coined it in December of 1985. Three runs in six innings? That's a 4.50 ERA! In what world is that a measure of quality?

Let's start with that criticism. It's true that 3 x 9 / 6 = 4.5. (You came here for this sort of high-level math, right?) But it's also true that type of start, meeting the bare minimum for earning a quality start, is unusual. Here's the proportion of quality starts in which the pitcher lasted exactly six innings and yielded exactly three earned runs. (I'm going to confine this analysis to the 30-team era, 1998-present. Almost all data retrieved in this article is via the Baseball-Reference Play Index.)

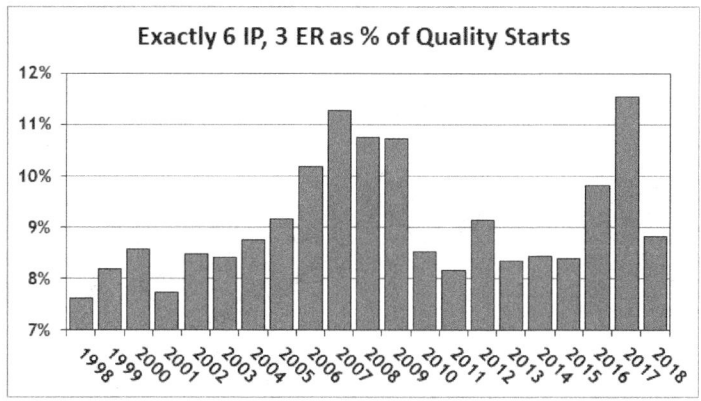

There were 1,997 quality starts in 2018. Only 176, or fewer than one in 11, featured a pitcher going six innings and allowing three earned runs. Put another way, the percentage of quality starts that resulted in a 4.50 ERA (8.8 percent) is less than half the percentage of games in which a batter hit two home runs and his team lost (22.5 percent; 237-69 won-lost). That doesn't impugn hitting two homers.

So if a 4.50 ERA isn't the norm, what is? How good are quality starts?

Pretty good, it turns out. First, on a team level:

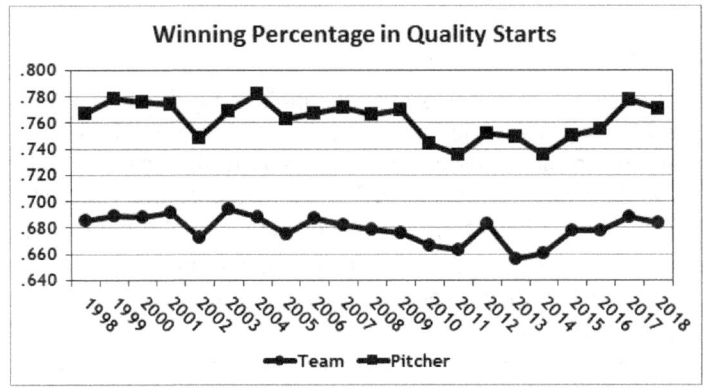

Teams receiving a quality start from their pitcher won 68.4 percent of their games in 2018, in line with the 30-team era average of 67.9 percent. A team with a .684 winning percentage wins 111 games. Getting a quality start is definitely a good thing. Individual pitchers throwing quality starts have a higher winning percentage because a big slice of team losses is assigned to a reliever.

If teams do well in quality starts, how well do the starting pitchers do? Again, very well.

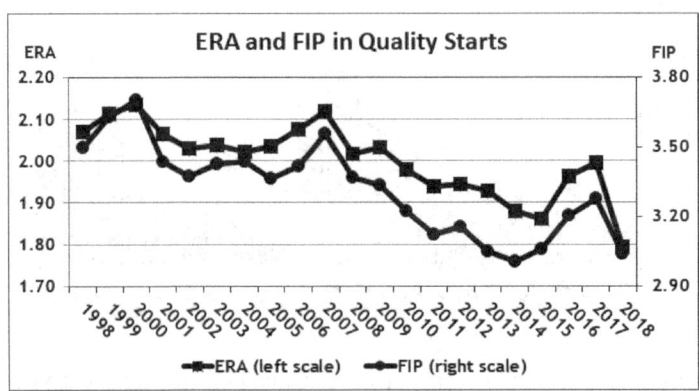

Pitchers in quality starts had a 1.79 ERA (blue line) in 2018, *the lowest in the 30-team era*. Their FIP was higher, 3.04, but still excellent. In the 30-team era, only 2014 had a lower FIP for quality starts, 3.01.

But, of course, the run environment in 2014 was different. Teams in 2014 scored 4.07 runs per game, the fewest in a non-strike year since 1976. They scored 4.45 runs per game in 2018. So surrendering a 3.04 FIP in 2018 is more impressive than 3.01 in 2014. Accordingly, let's look at ERA and FIP in quality starts relative to league averages.

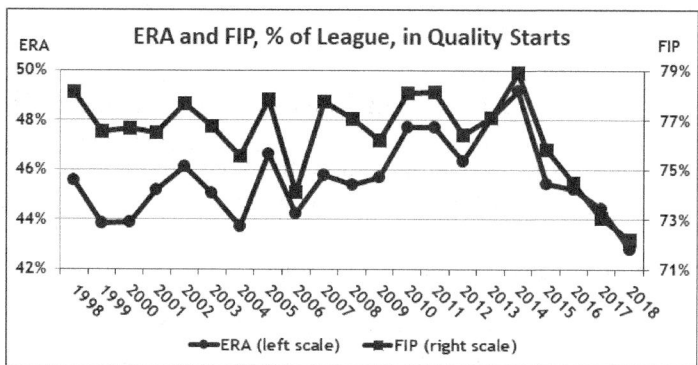

This tells a more dramatic story. Starting pitchers in 2018 gave up a 4.19 ERA and a 4.21 FIP. Starters in quality starts gave up a 1.79 ERA, 43 percent of the league average. Starters in quality starts gave up a 3.04 FIP, 72 percent of the league average. Both of these marks represent lows in the 30-team era.

The takeaway here is this: *Quality starts are better, relative to other starts, than they've ever been over the past 21 years.*

Maybe during the winter I'll look at this over a longer arc of time. For now, though, we can definitively say quality starts are the best they've ever been since the Diamondbacks and Rays joined the majors.

Yet, paradoxically, they're down.

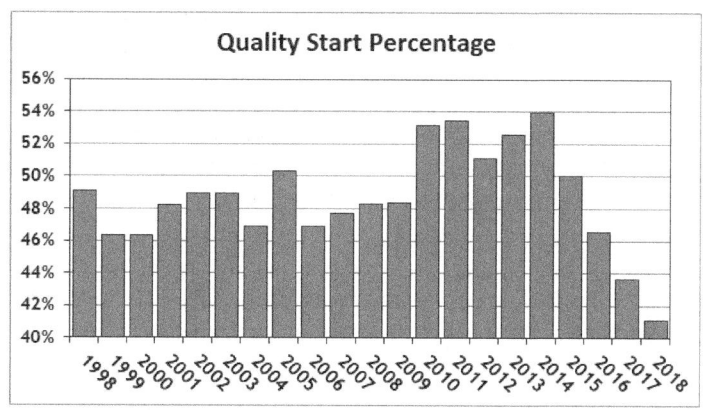

This graph covers only the 30-team era. In my article last week, though, I looked at the years 1908-2018. The result was the same. The 41 percent of starts in 2018 that were quality starts are an all-time low, well below the runners-up: 1930's 43 percent (the year teams scored an all-time record 5.55 runs per game) and last year's 44 percent.

The normal explanation for a dip in quality start percentage is an increase in scoring. When teams score a lot of runs, it's harder for starting pitchers to last six or more innings and limit opponents to three earned runs. From 1998 to 2014, the correlation between runs scored per game and the percentage of starts that were quality starts was -0.94. That means there was an extremely close relationship: More runs, fewer quality starts. Too small a sample? Go back to the start of the Expansion Era, 1961, and the relationship is even more negative, a -0.95 correlation, though 2014.

But that's broken down over the past four years:

- 2015: Runs per game increased from 4.07 to 4.25, quality start percentage decreased from 54.0 to 50.1. Yes, that's a negative relationship, but the regression model would predict a decline of 1.5 percentage points. We got 3.9 instead.
- 2016: Runs per game increased from 4.25 to 4.48, quality start percentage decreased from 50.1 to 46.6. Past experience would suggest a decline of just 1.8 percentage points. We got 3.4.
- 2017: Runs per game increased from 4.48 to 4.65, quality start percentage decreased from 46.6 to 43.6. Again, the direction's right, but the magnitude isn't. Using the relationship from 1998 to 2014, that increase in scoring should've reduced quality starts by 1.3 percentage points, not 2.9.
- 2018: Runs per game declined from 4.65 to 4.45. That should've resulted in the quality start percentage moving in the other direction, rising 1.6 points. It didn't. It fell 2.6 points, as noted, to an all-time low.

Granted, we're talking about just four years here. Maybe they're outliers. But I don't think they are. Quality starts, as noted, are as good or better than ever. But they're rarer than ever as well. And I think I know why.

To get a quality start, you need to allow three or fewer earned and pitch at least six innings. That's 18 outs. Here's a graph showing the number of starting pitchers who limited their opponents to three or fewer earned runs but got pulled after pitching at least five innings but fewer than six:

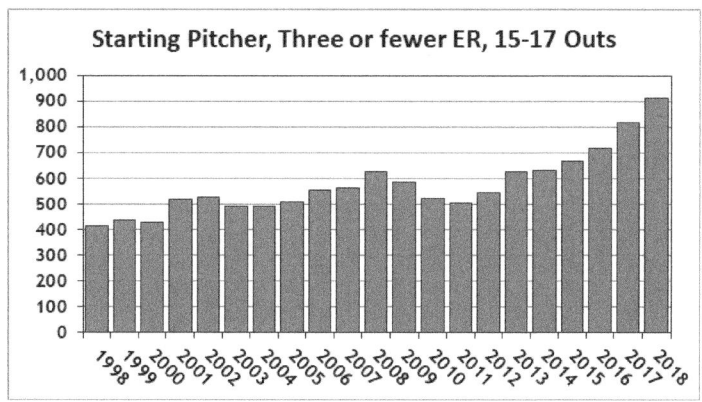

A pitcher getting 15 outs pitched five innings. A pitcher getting 16 outs pitched 5 1/3. A pitcher getting 17 outs pitched 5 2/3. More than ever before, pitchers are being removed from games in which they are within 1-3 outs of a quality start, falling just short of the six-inning finish line. Widespread acknowledgement of the times-through-the-order penalty and a flotilla of available bullpen arms is making the quality start simultaneously both more excellent and more rare.

Which is ironic, given that we saw a new post-war quality start record this season:

Rank	Pitcher	Season	Consecutive QS
1	Jacob deGrom	2018	24
2	Bob Gibson	1968	22
-	Chris Carpenter	2005	22
4	Johan Santana	2004	21
5	Luis Tiant	1968	20
-	Mike Scott	1986	20
-	Jake Arrieta	2015	20
8	Robin Roberts	1952	19
-	Tom Seaver	1973	19
-	Jack Morris	1983	19
-	Greg Maddux	1998	19
-	Josh Johnson	2010	19
-	Jon Lester	2014	19

While there have been longer streaks spread over multiple seasons, no pitcher since World War II threw more consecutive quality starts in one year than Jacob deGrom this year. The fact that he did in a year in which quality starts were the rarest they've ever been adds to the accomplishment.

—*Rob Mains is an author of Baseball Prospectus.*

Heads-Up Hacking—The First Pitch

Matthew Trueblood

Batters fell behind in a higher percentage of all plate appearances in 2018 than in any previous season for which we have pitch-by-pitch data. That kind of granular information goes back only to 1988, but we might safely assume (given all we know about baseball as it had been before that, and as it has been in the years since) that batters have *never* fallen behind at a higher rate than they did last season.

Through the 1990s, the percentage of all plate appearances that began 0-1 hovered in the high 30s and low 40s. In the 2000s, it rose steadily but slowly, through the mid-40s. In 2018, 49.8 percent of all trips to the plate began 0-1. That, as much as anything, captures in microcosm the nature of hitting in MLB today.

A countdown clock toward strike three begins ticking almost the moment a batter takes his place in the box. The league's adjusted OPS+ on the first pitch was higher in 2018 than ever before, and that has been true in most of the last 10 seasons. Batters hit .264/.289/.442 in all plate appearances in which they swung at the first pitch last season, and .241/.330/.395 in all plate appearances in which they took that first offering.

The percentage differences in batting average and isolated power there favor swinging at the first pitch by more than in any season since 1988, while the difference in on-base percentage favors taking by more than ever. If you want to get on base at a decent clip, it's a good idea to be patient, but you run the risk of missing the only chances you'll get to produce power.

Arizona Diamondbacks 2019

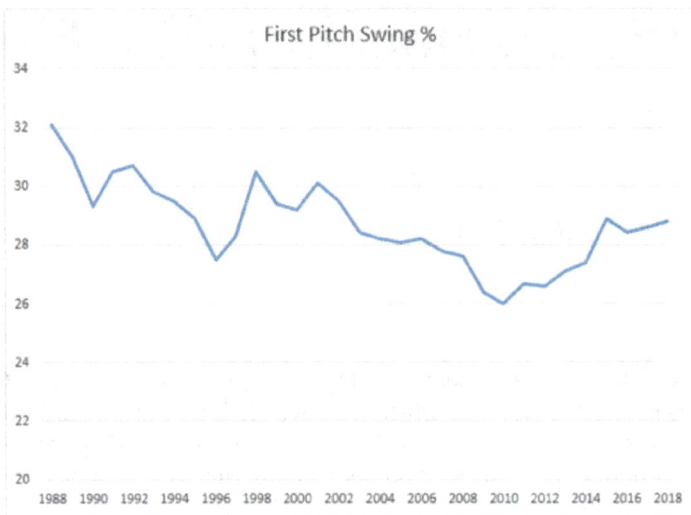

The league swung at the first pitch 28.8 percent of the time in 2018. With the isolated exception of 2015, that's the highest that number has climbed since 2002, but it might not be high enough. With the help of BP research maven Rob McQuown, I looked at the aggregate Called Strike Probability (CSProb) on the first pitch for each season since 2008, when the implementation of PITCHf/x first made measuring that possible. It's risen sharply during that period.

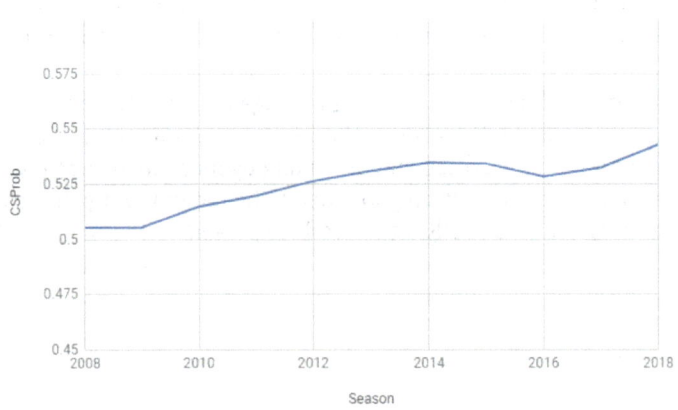

Called Strike Probability, First Pitch of PA (2008-2018)

Called Strike Probability is exactly what it sounds like: a pitch with a given CSProb has roughly that chance of being called a strike, if not swung at. In 2018, a batter who took 100 first pitches from a random sampling of the league's pitchers might expect to fall behind 54 or 55 times—up from 50 or 51 times in 2008. Almost regardless of pitch type (and, notably, especially in the case of fastballs), the first pitch tends to have more of the zone right now than ever before.

Pitchers are better at throwing strikes. They have better stuff, and believe more in their ability to miss bats within the zone. Perhaps most importantly, they know that batters are looking for one thing on the first pitch: a fastball. If they don't get it, they're likely to take the pitch. Check out how the use of sinkers and four-seamers on the first pitch has changed in a decade:

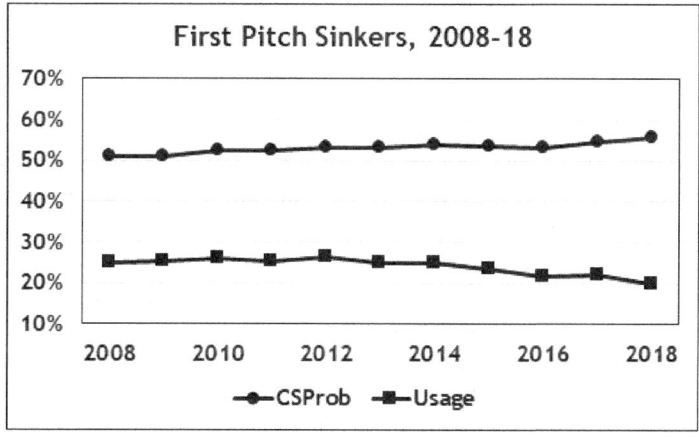

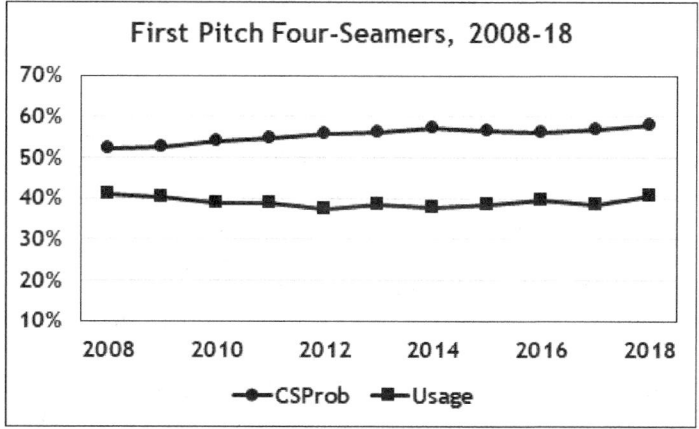

Heads-Up Hacking—The First Pitch - 113

The sinker is losing its place in baseball, but the rate at which pitchers have thrown it on the first pitch hasn't dropped any faster than its usage rate in other counts. Pitchers have actually gone to their four-seamer *more* often to open counts, in the last few years, after a dip in the 2012-2015 period. What's really changed, though, and what shows up in both charts above, is that pitchers are catching more of the zone with first-pitch fastballs than they were a decade ago, or a half-decade ago. They're attacking right away, even with the pitch they know batters are expecting. The message is pretty clear: batters are being too passive.

Sliders, curves, and changeups each have more of the zone when thrown on the first pitch than they did several years ago, too, though the effect is less pronounced. Pitchers have seen the numbers; they know batters are doing better on the first pitch itself. They still feel safe throwing more and better strikes than ever before, figuring they'll come out ahead as long as they keep getting ahead to open each battle.

The Moneyball revolution brought an increased league-wide focus on OBP, which resulted in a de facto mandate to take a more patient tack at the plate. It worked very well for a while, as batters with poor plate discipline were compelled to either adjust or be expelled from the league, and pitchers with poor control were slowly weeded out.

However, concurrent with that revolution, and spurred by it in some ways, was the evolution of the pitching paradigm that now dominates the game. As batters ratcheted up their focus on inflating pitch counts and working walks, pitchers honed theirs on throwing strikes and missing bats. The league's understanding of what makes a good pitcher improved at least as much, from the mid-1990s through the mid-2000s, as its understanding of what makes a good hitter. As amphetamines and other performance-enhancing drugs were phased mostly out of the game, and as PITCHf/x broke onto the scene, individuals and teams learned how to exploit the evolved approaches of even the smartest hitters.

The ability to avoid making outs is still the most valuable one in baseball, but the magnitude of its eclipse of slugging is smaller than ever. To a greater extent than power, on-base skills derive their value from chaining—from the on-base skill levels of the players on either side of a given individual. Eleven years ago, when the housing crisis hit, people learned the hard way that the value of their homes depended a good deal on the values of their neighbors' homes. The same wasn't true, though, of their cars. So it is now, with OBP and SLG.

The global OBP in 2018 was .318. The only seasons since the Dead Ball Era in which the league got on base at a worse clip were 2013-2015, 1988, 1971-1972, and 1963-1968. This is all happening despite the aforementioned evolution of the science of hitting. It's happening despite a shift in approach and focus, one that would steer OBP ever higher, if only it were working.

Instead, it's sitting at a low ebb, and while it does so, even guys who get on base often are a little less helpful than they were 10 years ago—or 20, or 40, or 60, or 70, or 80, or 90. They're less helpful, that is, because unless there happen to be three or four other guys in the lineup who get on just as regularly, their contribution is merely to forestall the inevitable. Runs happen, increasingly, when a sudden bang happens, and that means attacking early in the count—because pitchers are sure as hell doing that.

In a league making contact on barely 75 percent of its swings, and a league in which an increasing number of pitchers can throw multiple off-speed pitches for strikes in any count, the only way to consistently generate offense is going to be aggressive. This isn't necessarily true for individuals, like Mookie Betts and Jose Ramirez, who make a lot of contact and have excellent plate discipline, and whose power comes from such natural quickness in a short stroke. Most players have to make tradeoffs, though, whether it be lowering their contact rate or raising their chase rate, in order to consistently make the quality of contact necessary to survive in today's game.

Highest %	Lowest %
Javier Baez – 48.3	Joe Mauer – 4.6
Freddie Freeman – 47.1	Mookie Betts – 9.7
Ozzie Albies – 46.3	Brett Gardner – 10.7
Jose Altuve – 44.2	Jose Ramirez – 12.0
Nick Castellanos – 44.1	Jason Kipnis – 13.8
Joey Gallo – 42.3	Jesus Aguilar – 14.5
Corey Dickerson – 40.9	Xander Bogaerts – 15.8
Salvador Perez – 40.8	Brian Dozier – 16.3
Eddie Rosario – 40.7	Mike Trout – 17.6
Nick Ahmed – 40.4	Yasmani Grandal – 17.6

Top 10 and Bottom 10 Hitters, First-Pitch Swing Rate (2018)

The question isn't which of these lists one prefers, but what they each convey, qualitatively, about the cat-and-mouse game of early-count hitting. Those top five on the left, especially, drive home the fact that for most players, getting aggressive early in the count is now key to keeping strikeout rate down and hitting for power.

For now, the message is: pitchers are coming right after batters with the nastiest stuff they've ever had. Batters had better stop giving away strike one and force hurlers to adjust, or the global OBP crisis is only going to get worse.

—*Matthew Trueblood is an author of Baseball Prospectus.*

A Hymn for the Index Stat

Patrick Dubuque

We survived without computers. I know this, because I remember the day when my dad hooked up his brand-new Atari 400 computer to the back of our 12-inch Magnavox television, and the perfect blue of the memo pad lit up for the first time. I was born just on the edge of that transitional generation, of learning cursive and balancing checkbooks and just doing math all the time, constant manual arithmetic.

It still amazes me. We learned how to sail ships without computers. We learned how to do calculus. We built towers that didn't fall down, most of the time. We engineered catapults to knock them down anyway. We built a robust system of philosophy called "utilitarianism," founded on the principle that the good of an action is evaluated by summing the effects of that action, which is the kind of formula that would make the world's mainframes crash. The whole foundation of statistics as a field is "here's math you could easily do but would die of old age first."

The fact of the matter is that there is too much math in the world to do. There are too many things changing, and too many things too small to notice, for us to handle. At some point, they become too much for the computers to handle as well, which is why we have chaos theory and undetectable earthquakes, but it's not an even fight. At some point, we fall back on intuition, and given how under-equipped we are, we're forced to bestow that intuition with some sort of supernatural superiority, the "gut feeling," that we can't prove because we can only intuit that our intuition is better.

We're all lousy at intuition, and wonderful at lying to ourselves about it. The honest truth is that computers are far better at intuition than we are, because in order to know what feels "off" you have to know what's "on." In order to do that you have to constantly reassess the average of everything, then re-rank your own experience against it.

Test your own, by comparing these three anonymous lines:

Player	G	HR	AVG	OBP	SLG
Player A	156	38	.259	.342	.535
Player B	154	38	.280	.348	.527
Player C	158	38	.266	.343	.509

These all seem like pretty similar players, right? The second one a touch more batted-ball dependent, the third a little less strong, but all pretty good hitters. And you'd be right, about the latter. Not the former.

Here's the breakdown:

- Player A: 1991 Howard Johnson, 141 DRC+
- Player B: 1996 Dean Palmer, 121 DRC+
- Player C: 2018 Giancarlo Stanton, 114 DRC+

Baseball is fortunate to have escaped the seismic shifts of so many other sports, where the talents and performances of other eras are nearly unrecognizable. (And not just other sports: try to explain the greatness of the movie Duck Soup without adjusting for era.) But they're still there, and they're nearly impossible to account for manually, without having to resort to sweeping generalizations like "steroid era" or juiced-ball era" to throw out entire swathes of production.

This is all to say that we should celebrate the index stat, that simple 100-based scale with such a humble aim: just to give context. It's hard to imagine how we lived without them for so long. Sabermetricians have always tried to make their stats look like other stats: True Average mapped to batting average, FIP molded to look like and compare to ERA. It's easy to understand the motivation—these statistics carry an emotional value in them that is hard to resist, as with the .300 hitter and the 2.00 ERA—but even they fall prey to the same loss of scale as their unadjusted counterparts. If a .300 average means different things in different years, does that hold true for a .300 True Average?

Instead, 100 doesn't say anything, except above average or below. And it does it instantly, for every season in every run environment for any statistic we want it to. We should have more index stats: K%+, so we can stop comparing Mike Clevinger's career 9.46 K/9 to Nolan Ryan's 9.55. HBP%+, so we can note that Ron Hunt was getting plunked when nobody else was getting plunked, as opposed to that imitator Brandon Guyer. Some might note how stale these references are and accuse league-adjustment as a backward-looking drive, and this is true. But we're always looking backward, always comparing the new with the expectations already set. The index stat just forces us to be honest.

There's always resistance to a new statistic, especially one so outwardly simple and so internally complex. We tend to stick with what we know, even in the case of formulas that are supposed to tell us what we know. But if your resistance is that it seems too complicated, too counterintuitive, too "black boxy," I encourage you to consider why you feel that way. Because the real world is infinitely more complicated than baseball, where all the pitches go in one basic direction and the baserunners are only allowed to travel in four directions. Baseball statistics based on mixed methodology are almost impossibly intricate. So are skyscrapers and automobiles. That's why we have computers—to take the guesswork out of them.

—*Patrick Dubuque is an author of Baseball Prospectus.*

Index of Names

Ahmed, Nick	20	Marte, Ketel	34
Alexander, Blaze	85, 93	McCarthy, Jake	72, 93
Andriese, Matt	42	McFarland, T.J.	60
Avila, Alex	22	Mercer, Matt	87
Barrosa, Jorge	85	Miller, Jared	87
Bracho, Silvino	44	Murphy, John Ryan	36
Bradley, Archie	46	Peralta, David	38
Brito, Socrates	85	Perdomo, Geraldo	73, 95
Chafin, Andrew	48	Ray, Robbie	62
Chisholm, Jazz	70, 89	Refsnyder, Rob	85
Clarke, Taylor	80, 96	Robinson, Kristian	74, 90
Cron, Kevin	85	Rzepczynski, Marc	87
Duplantier, Jon	81, 90	Scott, Robby	87
Dyson, Jarrod	24	Sherfy, Jimmie	64, 96
Ellis, Drew	85	Shipley, Braden	87
Escobar, Eduardo	26	Smith, Pavin	75, 94
Flores, Wilmer	28	Souza, Steven	40
Godley, Zack	50	Szczur, Matt	85
Greinke, Zack	52	Tabor, Matt	87
Hirano, Yoshihisa	54	Thomas, Alek	85, 92
Holland, Greg	56	Tomas, Yasmany	76
Jones, Adam	30	Tomlinson, Kelby	85
Joseph, Caleb	85	Vargas, Emilio	87
Kelly, Carson	71	Vargas, Ildemaro	77
Kelly, Merrill	82	Varsho, Daulton	78, 91
Koch, Matthew	58	Walker, Christian	85
Krehbiel, Joseph	87	Walker, Taijuan	66
Lamb, Jake	32	Weaver, Luke	68
Lewicki, Artie	87	Widener, Taylor	84, 92
Leyba, Domingo	85, 95	Wilson, Marcus	85, 96
Lopez, Yoan	83, 95	Yerzy, Andy	79, 97

Ballpark diagrams for Baseball Prospectus are created by THIRTY81Project, a design concept offering original ballpark artwork, including the new 'Ballparks of 2019' 11 x 17 color print.

Visit **www.thirty81project.com** for full details.